Organising for Local Government:

a local political responsibility

by

John Barratt and John Downs

General Editors: Michael Clarke and John Stewart

Longman

in association with the Local Government Training Board

Longman Group UK Limited
Longman House, Burnt Mill, Harlow, Essex CM20 2JE
© Longman Group UK Ltd, 1988

First published 1988

British Library Cataloguing in Publication Data
Barratt, John
    Organising for local Government. — (Managing
    local government).
    1. Great Britain. Local government.
    Management
    I. Title   II. Downs, John   III. Clarke,
    Michael   IV. Stewart, John, *1929 Mar. 19–*
    V. Local Government Training Board
    VI. Series
    352.041

ISBN 0-581-02555-9

Typeset by Tradeset Limited, Welwyn Garden City, Herts
Printed by Bell and Bain Ltd., Glasgow

Dedication

The authors are indebted to many people who, wittingly or unwittingly, have contributed to the making of this book. To them and, in particular, to Robert James and Hugh Little — men from different political backgrounds and leaders of two very different local authorities, whose committed leadership and belief in the value of robust local government made it possible for us to help their local authorities to help themselves — this book is dedicated.

Contents

Editors' Foreword

This book is one of the first in a new management series launched by the *Local Government Training Board* to be published by *Longman Group UK Ltd*. The series is designed to help those concerned with management in local government to meet the challenges of the next few years. It is based on the belief that in no period has it been so important for local authorities to have effective management.

The impact of government legislation is clear. Each local authority has to review its management, if it is to achieve an effective response. But the challenge is much deeper. In a changing society, new problems and issues demand from local authorities a capacity to respond in new ways. Local authorities have to become closer to their public as customer and citizen; resources have to be managed to achieve value in service; the requirement on all authorities is to achieve effective management of the changes which are taking place.

Effective management requires effective management development. The series is designed to aid the management development of present and future officers — and councillors. It is designed to be *used* by the reader in a variety of situations. While we hope that the books will be used on local government management courses we hope that they will have a much wider use.

They can be used by individuals or groups of managers or as the basis of seminars within authorities. However, the series will truly be a success if it becomes regarded as resource material for use in the business of management itself. We hope that the ideas discussed and the experience pooled will be a stimulus to more effective management.

The series is based on two principles. The first is the need for even greater emphasis on developing effective management in local government and the constant search for improvement. The second is that effective management must take account of the nature of local government. Need for effective management has already been stressed: the case for a separate series particular to local government is based on our second principle.

There are plenty of management books. What we have set out to produce is a series geared to the particular needs of local government. We would want to argue that those concerned with management in local government should draw on as wide a range of general experience as possible. Furthermore we would also want to agree that proper account is taken of the special purposes, conditions and tasks of local government. These books will help the manager to do just that. In publishing them we are not pretending that there is *one right way* to manage a local authority. Rather, we are exposing ideas and questions to help fashion the most helpful and effective approach to the local situation.

The first books in the sequence serve both to introduce the series and to highlight some of the key issues facing management in local authorities. The series will be extended by covering other issues of contemporary concern which require to be tackled if management — and the health of the local authority — is to be improved.

Michael Clarke, Director, Local Government Training Board
Professor John Stewart, Institute of Local Government Studies

Introduction

Why this book?

This book is about organisational health in a local authority — a subject important at any time, but never more so than now. An 'artificial person' like a local authority is given practical expression through its visible organisation and through the work of the people elected to it or employed by it. If the developing challenges of a rapidly changing community are to be faced effectively, the local authority's organisation must be purposefully adapted also. The goal of effective local democracy cannot be achieved if the local authority's efforts are confined within organisational arrangements which are under strain because they still seek to provide what have developed into nationally significant public services through nationally organised professions on the basis of national political dogmas and rivalries. Such a situation will merely reflect a local version of national politics and practices rather than the specific local concerns of a local community expressed and dealt with through the local council.

Local councillors are there to create and implement their own collective local political agenda and to influence those national public services, which their predecessors helped to develop from local origins, in pursuit of that local agenda.

What is the challenge?

How, we ask, can councillors move away from their seemingly unbreakable tradition of minor executive decision-making in relation to the institutionalised traditional local authority services? How can the council be helped to concentrate instead on choosing and pursuing the local issues to be tackled based on its assessment of the needs of the local community? How can the council control its 'in-house' services? How can it influence the independent agencies which contribute to the success, or otherwise, of the council's chosen strategies? How can the council, in its dealings with central government, maximise its own power on local issues, minimise the distraction of national political issues, and manage a constructive tension about the issues which have inevitably to be negotiated through the middle of the national/local contest for power?

The book seeks to answer these questions. It is constructed round the concept of a 'local political agenda' and the importance of consciously organising the resources of a local authority in a way which enables such an agenda to be articulated and implemented.

Some starter questions for the reader

The target readers of this book are local authority elected members (the councillors) and senior employees, whatever their political or professional background. Its objective is to engage the reader in recognition, which can then be shared with fellow councillors and employees, of organisational problems and opportunities, and of practical ways of making progress. The following questions may help you find the parts of the book most relevant to your needs. Think about them now and note down your answers for use when you read the relevant chapters.

1. Are you unsure about the purpose of your local
   authority and whether it is fully exercising its role?   Chapters 1 and 2
2. Is your council geared to developing and
   controlling its own political agenda?   Chapters 3 and 5
3. Is there a clearly and purposefully defined local
   political agenda?   Chapters 4 and 6
4. Do the council's committees and employees follow
   the council's sense of direction?   Chapters 6, 7 and 8
5. Is the council effectively supported by its
   employees?   Chapters 5, 7 and 8
6. Does the council systematically plan and review
   performance in the achievement of its agenda?   Chapter 9
7. Are councillors able to do their jobs properly?   Chapter 10
8. Is organisational change needed but difficult to
   achieve?   Chapter 11

How to use this book

Our basic proposition, and the reason for anyone persevering as a reader, is that the organisational health and vitality of a local authority cannot be left to a mixture of history and chance: it has to be worked at. So throughout the book we provide means for readers to evaluate their satisfaction with the position in which they judge their own organisation to be.

Of the questions we have just asked, only one or two may have prompted a response. Going straight to a particular chapter may well be the best way for a busy and preoccupied reader. As the concepts behind each chapter are inter-related, you can work outwards from your chosen point of entry or read right through a whole sequence.

The route through the book is one which develops from the general to the particular — becoming increasingly more focused on specific way of analysing the local situation and taking appropriate action. In the earlier chapters we try to argue from first principles and establish a stance on the role and imperatives for local authorities in the future. With a rationale thus established and, we hope, shared by the reader we then begin to lay down some propositions, tests and chal-lenges to enable you to respond positively — to agree or disagree, to sketch out conclusions and action which should be taken.

To encourage action, each chapter contains some examples of good practice and other promptings, to be compared with the reader's own circumstances. Each chapter begins with a summary and ends with some questions to focus the reader's attention on likely targets for action. In answering the questions, make up your own mind first about your answers and then compare what you have decided with what your colleagues think. They are intended to encourage both self-questioning and dialogue. Even if the specific suggestions for organisational improvement which we make are not accepted, our insistence that there must be a shared aware-ness of, and investment in, the importance of organisational health as a political and operational priority should strike a chord with the increasing number of people who are concerned about 'effectiveness' as well as 'efficiency'. We have introduced, therefore, some terminology, concepts, examples and questions as a means of further developing that shared awareness, which we hope will be of positive value. We have avoided generalised blueprints and point to some useful starting points for local reflection, and action related to local needs. The questions — like the book itself — are meant to be challenging, and some may find them overfacing. But they are not a formal examination and in many cases you will be quite entitled to respond 'I don't know'! Relax, but ponder the problems the questions raise — then look for allies in thinking through and solving them. We cannot be blamed for the organisation we inherit, but we do have a responsibility to try to keep it relevant to current concerns. Although the authors' personal prejudices are bound to be apparent, we have tried to make the book value-free on matters of political choice, with the key exception of organisational health as itself a claimant for priority treatment. By simplifying what appears overwhelmingly complex, by highlighting the key levers which control the mass of detail, and by offering clear starting points for analysis and remedial action in the theme of each chapter, the book should stimulate those who know they have a responsibility for organisational excellence but do not know how to make progress.

Because its constant advice is to get the starting points right, and to delegate the consequences, the book is not put to best use in judging what other people should be doing. Whether you are a councillor or an employee of a local authority the book should be related to your level of responsibility so that you can assess whether changes are needed in the working practices and arrangements which you can influence or amend in your locality.

Most successful changes in culture, in collaboration or in arrangements, begin in a small way and expand their success because of their success. As the council seeks to make an impact on ever-changing local social, economic and environmental circumstances, so the people who matter in the organisation must be prepared to change the arrangements which affect themselves. Of course, if your job in the organisation doesn't matter — it is time it changed anyway!

The fundamental principles of organisational effectiveness which the book discusses are of universal validity. Readers from other backgrounds should find it useful to see how those principles can be applied to the unique setting of a local authority and draw their own parallels.

Sequence of arguments and chapters

In Chapter 1 we explore the constitutional purposes of a local authority in the British national systems of self-government. Present challenges can be met more calmly if they can be seen in the context of history and of fundamental purposes which are consciously accepted. In Chapter 2 we analyse the components of the organisation and the impact of the individual people involved in them. Chapter 3 examines the stages by which the organisation can be re-shaped.

If the organisation is to fulfil the council's will, the council must make that will clear in operationally meaningful terms, so Chapter 4 suggests practical ways of determining the council's overall local political agenda for which the organisation must then be designed.

The scale and complexity of the council's responsibilities are such that they require carefully organised support if its local political agenda is to be directed at the right priorities and implemented effectively, so Chapter 5 examines the question 'Who are the people who should be advising the council about its local community, about its options and about its progress?' Unless this critically important role is loyally and determinedly undertaken, the council will find it difficult to express and to impose its collective will effectively.

Chapter 6 looks at implementation of the council's will and poses the question 'Who is accountable for achieving the results which the council wants?' This is a very different standpoint than 'running a department' or 'providing a service'.

One option likely to be chosen as a means of implementation (often for reasons of tradition rather than effectiveness) is that of an 'in-house' professional organisation, whether advisory or operational, within a relevant department. Chapter 7 explores the need for clear 'top down' management to prevent the sheer weight of traditional 'in-house' activities determining the council's actual direction.

In any organisation, its people are important. Their skills, commitment and behaviour are the determining factors in the use of the council's other resources of legal powers, money and property. In the work of a democratically controlled organisation that importance should be underlined, yet the standard of the arrangements for encouraging and enabling people to give of their best in a local authority is usually not very high. Chapter 8 highlights the challenge to motivate people.

Chapter 9 explores a challenge which local authorities must meet. Measuring and managing performance does go on, to some extent, in all local authorities, but rarely is it practised systematically and universally or as a normal part of the overall cycle of management. Yet without it the council will be steering blind and having to resort to random checks on the current state of affairs which will clog and warp the decision-making processes. Measuring achievement is a challenge which must be vigorously taken up if local authorities are to be able to demonstrate their worth.

Chapter 10 asks whether councillors' time is used by the organisation to best effect, in what roles and using what skills. We assert that councillors should have defined jobs to do, just as much as officers, and should be consciously deployed, developed and appraised. We publish the first job descriptions ever of a chairman and of a councillor in terms of the results they have to achieve, and invite them to plan and appraise their own performances, not least in working together with other councillors and senior employees in finding common ground and caring for the health of their organisation, in order to secure local progress and a future for the notion of governing locally.

Chapter 11 encourages the reader, who feels a need for local action, to start the ball rolling.

So, away with internalised games about status and rivalry, of labyrinthine processes to produce ineffective results, of layers of patchwork co-ordination to supplement inadequate and rigid traditional structures, of mountains of insufficiently digested detailed paperwork — the signs of a purposeless organisation concerned only with its own survival — and on to the fulfilment of basic purposes, by using the freedom to organise with courage, skill and determination.

1 What are we organising for?

Local authorities are only one of several ways of providing local government. It is their political role, rather than service management, which makes them distinctive. Does the council's organisation reflect its determination to be successful as a local means of solving local problems? Or has it become dominated by the details of service management? Creating and maintaining an effective organisation is vital for the successful fulfilment of the *local political agenda*.

Public accountability, exploration of issues and executive action should all be inter-related, but may require different forms of organisation to be successfully dealt with. Experiments take place in several local authorities but organisational health should be a constant, overall, political priority in every authority. Organisational arrangements are complex and costly, determining what the council can actually achieve. Careful and consistent organisational development must be based on sound information about the existing organisation and a realistic appreciation of the available options for change.

Local authorities and local government are not necessarily the same things

Local authorities have had a dominant place in the provision of local self-government in the United Kingdom for a century and a half. Their place in the unwritten constitution has become so well established that many people (including the authors of official reports) treat the phrases 'local government' and 'local authorities' interchangeably. No political party openly and directly proposes the general abolition of local authorities and many, if not most, have a stability of organisation which seems to assume a permanence unthreatened by its possible irrelevance to current social needs.

Yet behind this facade there is an increasing concern that all is not well. Quite apart from a procession of committees of inquiry and commissions which have separately pronounced upon different, yet related, questions about the stucture, finance and internal management of local authorities, and a sequence of more recent major legislation about them, there are the evident centralising tendencies of individual ministers in relation to the historic local authority services. The future role of local authorities was a major theme in the 1987 general election, and although the overall organisational implications of proposals were not much in evidence, the government's legislative programme appears to reject the notion of the local authority as the normal channel of local government in favour of other methods of local service delivery.

Not only is the direct pressure on the work of local authorities from central government increasing, but alternative ways of providing local government are being tried. Urban Development Corporations, Regional Water Authorities, the Manpower Services Commission, for example, have all operated in the decentralised provision, on behalf of central government, of what had previously been the devolved functions of local authorities.

Democratically elected, multi-purpose, local authorities with independent powers of taxation may have become an accepted, even normative, method of local government but their continued future is, in practice, very much under question. Some people, steeped in only the recent traditions of local authorities (traditions which were largely created during the grant-led expansion of the sixties) may be affronted by this questioning. Yet the fact is that Parliament, at the instigation of the government of the day, has constantly amended the terms on which local authorities have been authorised to operate, ever since the 1835 Municipal Corporations Act effectively inaugurated the modern era of local government.

This is clearly illustrated by the 'Chronological table of local government' compiled for the book *A Century of Municipal Progress*[1]. This was published to celebrate the centenary of the 1835 Act and is still essential reading for anyone wishing to understand the history that has shaped our current systems. Local government, in one form or another, has for centuries been a strong feature of our self-government; local authorities, in their current service roles, have not.

Widdicombe describes the attributes of local authorities as 'pluralism, participation and responsiveness'

Given these challenges, the question 'Why have local authorities?' is one which now needs to be asked explicitly and answered explicitly if there is to be a rational framework of governmental systems within which effective, democratic, local government is efficiently provided. The answer must obviously emerge from political debate, with the enthusiasts for local authorities vigorously putting forward clear and rational arguments which emphasise the special value a local authority represents.

What value can be added to the country-wide framework of government by the existence of local authorities? How far is that value being added in practice? How much greater is that value than alternative options for service delivery? That there are existing and potential alternatives to local authorities for the delivery of public services should never be forgotten. Do local authorities provide value beyond merely being an agent of service provision?

The Widdicombe Report[2] examined the claim of the Redcliffe-Maud Report[3] that 'Local Government [*sic*] is more than the sum of the particular services provided. It is an essential part of English democratic government.' Questioning whether that claim was still valid, Widdicombe asked what is the unique value which a democratically elected, multi-purpose, tax-levying, local authority represents? Widdicombe's answer[4] conveniently summarises three attributes of a local authority from which this value stems:

▽ 'pluralism, through which it contributes to the national political system;
▽ participation, through which it contributes to local democracy;

▽   responsiveness, through which it contributes to the provision of local needs
through the delivery of services'.

The principal distinguishing feature, then, of a local authority as an instrument of local government is its political role as a result of the members of the council being directly elected by the local electorate. They are not delegates, agents or
appointees of central government. So, although the council's formal powers are
given by Parliament, the councillors' collective powers to exercise these powers
stem from their direct election. In turn, local authority employees are directly
employed by 'the council', owing loyalty in their work to the council and not to
the government. The powers of a local authority are devolved, rather than decentralised, at any rate in theory and original intention, but the various ways in which
they have been circumscribed now cause considerable confusion as to what those
powers actually are. Despite this confusion, no one who has worked in, or been
elected to, a local authority will doubt the real pressures of direct election in
moulding the values and outlook of councillors and senior employees alike.

Our challenge is for local authorities to influence their organisational arrangements so that they support the Widdicombe attributes of pluralism, participation
and responsiveness which flow from the local electoral processes. The arguments
for having local authorities must be matched by their demonstrable achievements.

Local political processes are often obscured by poor organisation

The Widdicombe analysis firmly emphasises that the overriding function of a
local authority is to provide a competent local, political process. The efficient provision of locally sensitive services can be very important for such a process, but
only a consequence of it, nonetheless. The process itself still remains important
and valid despite changes, or even shrinkages, in the powers of direct service provision. The direct provision of a service is only one option available for implementing a council's responses to local problems. As the control of historic local
authority services is increasingly centralised, local authorities will need increasingly to improve both their political processes for identifying and dealing with
local issues and the range of methods still available to them, if they are to act on
behalf of the local community. The trouble is that the pursuit of a genuine *local
political agenda* appropriate to current times is obstructed by the unchallenged
practices, the compromises, the conventions and the partial solutions to the political and operational problems which we inherit from the past. The work of local
authorities is dominated by what have become fairly standard services, provided
increasingly in response to the national political agenda, and through the agency
of national networks of professional bodies. This is the reality and, coupled with
the inevitable tensions which follow from the unclear and ragged allocation of
responsibilities between central and local government, it obscures the importance
of the *local political agenda* as the basis of a local authority's life and thwarts its
proper organisation. Hasn't the time come for each local authority to assert its fundamental role by realistically appraising its current circumstances and reshaping
its internal arrangements to achieve maximum local effect? Why should it go on
wasting time in seeking to perpetuate the old order of things now only represented
by nominal responsibility for the local provision of national services? What new
opportunities are meanwhile being missed for meeting the *local political agenda*
through the various local services and agencies?

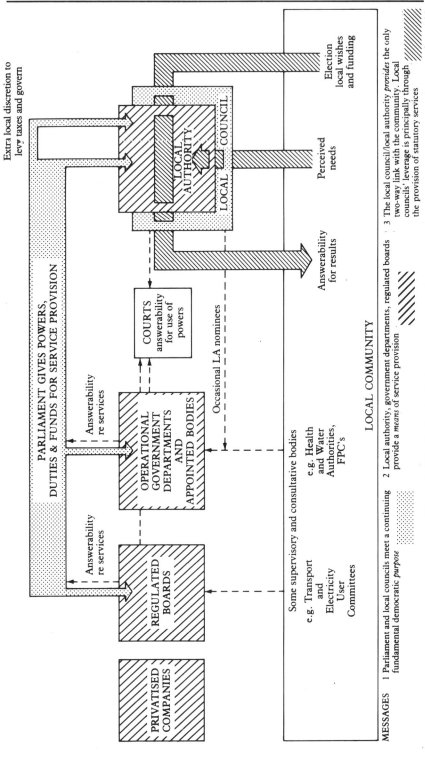

Figure 1. The distinction between purpose and means

MESSAGES   1 Parliament and local councils meet a continuing fundamental democratic *purpose*

2 Local authority, government departments, regulated boards provide a *means* of service provision

3 The local council/local authority *provides* the only two-way link with the community. Local councils' leverage is principally through the provision of statutory services

PARLIAMENT GIVES POWERS, DUTIES & FUNDS FOR SERVICE PROVISION

Extra local discretion to levy taxes and govern

LOCAL AUTHORITY

LOCAL COUNCIL

Election local wishes and funding

Perceived needs

Answerability for results

COURTS answerability for use of powers

Answerability re services

Answerability re services

OPERATIONAL GOVERNMENT DEPARTMENTS AND APPOINTED BODIES

REGULATED BOARDS

PRIVATISED COMPANIES

Occasional LA nominees

Some supervisory and consultative bodies

e.g. Transport and Electricity User Committees

e.g. Health and Water Authorities, FPC's

LOCAL COMMUNITY

Local authorities are in competition with other forms of local government so they need to justify their existence by the way they exert their influence

Figure 1 puts the local authority in context as but one of the means through which public services are provided. Other means include government departments providing operational services, from social security to land registration; appointed bodies such as development corporations and water and health authorities, or regulated boards such as electricity — to say nothing of the deregulated bus industry or British Gas or Telecom. Local authorities are but one means of giving service though some, in addition to the standard services, provide transport undertakings, some provide funeral chapels and even, as in Hull, a municipal telephone service. The fact that local councils are empowered by Parliament to provide certain services does give them significant leverage to effect priorities and styles of operation appropriate to local needs, but it is not the only dominant reason for their existence. In some cases, such as education, often described as 'a national service administered locally', there are strong arguments that such a service should be provided under the guidance and direction of a locally elected council. Why? Similarly it has been argued that some services, such as health, should be restored to local elected control — so important is it that they should be made sensitive to local needs. But would they? There are now arguments — and indeed legislation — to the contrary, and therein lies the challenge to local authorities to demonstrate the special value of their contribution to democracy.

The compelling argument for the existence of local authorities is their councillors' direct linkage with their local electorate, as depicted in Fig. 1 — in particular the implicit requirement upon them to assess local needs and wishes, and their answerability for making sensible judgments in due course being evaluated through the ballot box. Equally important is the extent to which the local electorate are substantial paymasters of the local authority. In the way they engage local democratic participation they are unique. The other 'means' of provision (by government departments, regulated boards etc.) lack that dimension and only nominally make up for it through consultative or user committees. Yet local authorities can have influence and demonstrate their value even here through the small number of seats to which they can nominate elected members — such as on family practitioner committees or community health councils. All too often, the local authority treats these opportunities for influence too lightly — mistaking them as peripheral to what it perceives as its main task, especially when their functions are less than riveting or their subjects impenetrable to the members appointed. How many elected members placed by their local authority on some of these bodies are sufficiently well briefed as to what they might be expected to achieve there — other than to attend and grind their individual axe, or act vaguely as a barometer of local opinion, or as monitors of the occasional issue of liaison required with their authority on some operational matter?

If the basic purpose of a local authority and its council is seen more as a mechanism for governing (by direct and indirect means) on local issues, then a clearer contrast can be demonstrated between the role of a local authority as a means of providing the local services on the one hand, and its role as the fulfiller of a fundamental purpose on the other hand, i.e. the purpose of local government.

Thus far then, four messages:

▽ the local council must govern, and that will not happen just by presiding over services;

▽ but a council's statutory ability and duty to provide services offers a powerful lever to exert local priorities;

▽ yet while local authorities assume their right to provide services, the justification for them to do this must be weighed in terms of the efficiency with which they provide the services, and the opportunity that is taken of ensuring that the services are responsive to local needs and opinion;

▽ a local authority's ability to influence — upwards to government, sideways to other authorities and agencies, and outwards to the community, employers etc. — is a lever capable of more exertion.

Local authorities are both a means to the end of sensitive service provision to the public, and also meet a fundamental democratic purpose of local government; and the latter is their predominant *raison d'être*. The way they organise themselves to achieve both is critical, but arguably the latter is the more critical, because if exercised powerfully it can mould to its will both its own services, those of others and developments in the world outside government.

So local authorities as a source of 'local government' (the popular name for 'local authorities') should become better at government and influence if they are to survive. In doing this they will be the more effective if they provide services efficiently, both as a vehicle for meeting their 'local political agendas' (democratically defined) and so that they can justify continued public trust in them as representative managers of those services for which the public pay.

To do this, councillors need to:

▽ set clear directions based on their *local political agenda*;
▽ use their power and influence to better effect;
▽ keep their eye on the main issues and off unimportant detail;
▽ engage themselves in continuing and rigorous performance review;
▽ promote their purpose and achievements better;
▽ ensure that their own and their senior staff's time, skills and energy are directed not just to purposeful management or to efficient administration, but in giving visionary direction and strong leadership.

In the Appendix we provide in Checklist One a means whereby you can audit where your own local authority now stands against these principles. In this way you can identify shortfalls and encourage new ideas and orientations in helping your council fulfil its potential and fully justify its claim to be local government. You might like to turn to page 118 now and pencil in your responses, before reading on . . .

The council can express its own mind through its organisation, given the will to do so

A local authority still has considerable freedom available to order its own organisation and internal processes in pursuit of its own objectives, but it needs the skill, patience and commitment of good leadership for that freedom to be fully utilised. It was the brave experiments and successful local initiatives by determined locally based commissioners of sewers, of lighting, of police etc. which caused Parliament to convert the old municipal corporations from being privately owned beneficial rights of property into the means of solving the monstrous problems of nineteenth-century industrialisation. Local initiative is still possible, even in a time of apparent decline. Indeed, the challenge to the worthwhileness of local authorities should be a major spur.

If local authorities are to meet the current needs of local communities which cannot be adequately dealt with by nationally standardised services, they will have to be less preoccupied with the day-to-day running of those services, because this tends to overshadow the creation, consideration and implementation of their genuine local agenda of current local concerns in a rapidly changing society. Indeed, unless they really can implement their local agenda through their residual powers over the traditional services, they will be living out a diversionary illusion by preserving an organisation and a political process which is increasingly appropriate only to the past. For example, concern for economic regeneration may well be a greater priority in the *local political agenda* than 'running' the standard services, yet this, and other major local issues which do not fit neatly into one of the traditional service boxes, may find itself as an organisational afterthought, struggling for practical recognition in the traditional departments, budgets and processes of an authority.

Because it is valuable to have a clear sense of purpose and mission as a plumbline with which to evaluate the validity, relevance and usefulness of the current organisation, we will be assuming the importance of determining and implementing '*the local political agenda*'. The emphasis which each local authority will seek to place on the relative significance of the three Widdicombe attributes — pluralism, participation and responsive service delivery — will vary from time to time and from each other. So, therefore, should the arrangements which give practical effect to that emphasis. The organisation then becomes the result of the local democratic process, instead of a picturesque heirloom of doubtful utility. What are the local issues which should be determined by local self-government? What are the wider issues which should be influenced by local self-government? What are the arrangements needed to identify, discuss, decide and implement this agenda?

The gap between the ideal and the existing situation, coupled with the many different attitudes of the people wielding actual power in the organisation, may turn the reader away from thoughts of taking action. Certainly a complete overhaul of the existing organisation will be a daunting, though worthwhile, task, but improvements can with advantage sometimes be made to discrete parts of the organisation, and some sufficiently agreed starting points for changes can usually be identified. Whatever the starting point or scale of entry, we suggest that the current challenge to the values of democratically elected local authorities is now too strong for any complacency about each individual authority's effectiveness. The best starting point for opening up the organisation to constructive change must surely be to take seriously the three Widdicombe attributes and ask:

▽   how is our organisation arranged to help the council contribute effectively to our country-wide political system? (the pluralism);
▽   how is our organisation arranged to help the council contribute effectively to local democracy? (the participation);
▽   how is our organisation arranged to contribute effectively to the meeting of local needs through the delivery of services? (the responsiveness).

In answering questions of this kind we need to consider the different kinds of business in which the council thus finds itself — the formal, the political and the executive.

The different kinds of business of a local council

Because the council is the sole source of authority for action taken by the local authority there must necessarily be an emphasis on the corporate role of councillors and a 'top down' stance if the council is to have any real control. The effect may therefore seem unduly centralist and unsympathetic to the needs of those numerous and important parts of the organisation which operate at a distance from the council, but that is not our intention. Extensive freedom to act by way of delegation must be met within a context of effective direction and control if the organisation is to avoid unnecessary conflict and to maximise opportunities for useful co-operation. Without clear overall policies, delegation will be thwarted as every controversial detail is taken to the highest possible level of decision-making.

In considering the responsibilities of the council it is worth recognising that there are at least three very different kinds of business undertaken and each requires a different kind of contribution from the people, elected or employed, whom the council involves. These different businesses are:

▽   in administration of the 'public body', exercising formal powers and duties, and fulfilling formal roles and relationships — the emphasis being on formal organisation;

▽   in processing the identification and meeting of local needs — the emphasis being on the political organisation;

▽   in securing managerial effectiveness and efficiency in service delivery — the emphasis being on the executive organisation.

These different kinds of business may require different choices to be made about how councillors and employees are organised to undertake them, yet most local authorities — and other public bodies — employ a single conventional and standardised format inherited from another age. This puts a heavy strain on their enthusiasms and energies as they struggle to make a relevant contribution to current problems. One councillor expressed a widely held view when he said that he felt 'trapped into processing other people's agendas'.

Administering the 'public body'

The first kind of 'business' — administering the 'public body', fulfilling obligatory functions, ensuring internal rules are fully observed, complying with legal requirements in the conduct of affairs and formally satisfying public demands for the formal treatment of particular issues or cases — is normally discharged through decisions made in formal session by a mix of councillors chosen by the council, or by the whole council itself. It is not unlike the concept of a jury of 'twelve good citizens and true', who will weigh the facts presented to them and come up with a common-sense answer. The meeting takes place regularly and has a procedure which ensures that the business is conducted in an orderly manner. It also takes place in public, because public accountability is an important factor, so there is a concern to be seen to get things right, rather than to explore in an open-ended way. The legalism and the openness of the situation are the dominant values. In any public body it is unlikely that this way of proceeding can be changed significantly, though improvements in location, presentation and timing can usefully be considered.

Processing the identification and meeting of local needs

The second kind of 'business' — of processing the identification and meeting of local needs — is concerned with such questions as 'what are the social, environmental, infrastructural and economic needs of the locality, what is their interrelationship, and what can the council do about them, directly or indirectly?' This requires a different approach, because big problems are involved which require well-thought-out policies, with implementation properly resourced and carefully planned and monitored. Informal discussions involving a wide range of people in free-ranging exploration of available options are desirable before clear choices are made in the public forum of a formal meeting. Frankness, lack of prejudice and adventurous thinking are needed if the open, formal process is to be well-informed and the inevitable problems of practical implementation are to be coped with efficiently and consistently. The informal arrangements are just as critical to success as the formal.

Securing managerial effectiveness and efficiency in service delivery

The third kind of 'business' — securing managerial effectiveness and efficiency in service delivery — requires the council to set clear objectives for those accountable to follow, with performance monitored to assist the council's control. Managerial effectiveness and efficiency are consequences of political choice and do not exist as ends in themselves. If there is no political backing for the achievement of impact through the work of a particular service, the most effective and efficient managerial action is to scrap that service. Yet so much time seems to be taken by councillors, on detailed executive work, instead of on setting the objectives that the real political business is thereby diminished. The council should be seen as the 'high command', engaged in winning a war, rather than a fragmented band of skirmishing tribes.

So the subject we will be exploring is the extent to which a council can improve its arrangements for implementing good local self-government through attention to three differing kinds of business requiring differing arrangements for each.

Local authorities deserve good organisational arrangements

This book is written out of a profound respect for the value of democratic local self-government and an appreciation of what is daily achieved by the hard work of many people, often in spite of the organisational arrangements imposed upon them. It is because many of these arrangements are open to criticism and change that the book concentrates hard on the likely deficiencies of a local authority's organisation, so that improvements can be made. Its criticisms are meant to be constructive and ought not to offend anyone conscientiously struggling to comprehend, co-ordinate and make relevant the use of the enormous resources which every day are committed by authority of the council on behalf of the local community. By raising the profile of organisational health as a topic which must itself be purposefully pursued, and by providing explanations of basic components and concepts which can be used to judge the value of existing arrangements, we are challenging to take experimental action those many councillors and senior employees who are increasingly concerned about the vigour of democratic local government at a time of both unprecedented changes in its relationships with central government and of challenge to current means of providing services. If a local authority cannot organise itself in seeking to cope effectively with current communal problems, what hope does it have of successful achievements on behalf of the local community? Control over its internal arrangements is a prerequisite to control over the many activities for which the council is responsible, and proof of that competence is surely a condition precedent before any widening of the scope of a local authority's influence could be contemplated by any government.

All the criticisms and practical suggestions in the book are based upon what has already been successfully put into practice in local authorities and with an eye to comparative experience in other parts of the public and private sectors. The widely held view, that much of what is wrong in local authorities stems directly from restrictions imposed by Parliament or central government, is an inadequate excuse for avoiding the challenge of what can be improved locally. In any event, any local experience of understanding and purposefully reshaping local arrangements will increase the chances of well-informed local contributions to any proposed or desirable national changes.

For those who doubt the extent of organisational change open to a local authority, it is interesting to compare the way the authority normally works (when its various activities are rarely held together and purposefully directed by a dominant set of current council instructions) with the way it responds to a major civil emergency — like a flood or an explosion — which suddenly affects the lives of many people. The sense of urgency to meet people's obvious needs overcomes the red tape, the departmental isolationism and in-fighting, and side-steps the traditional bureaucratic hierarchies and procedures. A leader is acknowledged and, for a brief time, the achievement of successful solutions is more important than status, internal rivalries and protocol. We have to ask why the problems for which the public pays to be tackled every day justify a less effective response than a temporary emergency!

Given the way in which its organisational arrangements will frequently decide the range of issues which the council considers, and the action which can be taken on its decisions, the importance of those arrangements is a major political priority for the council. The emphasis of the book is necessarily internalised and 'top down' to reflect that priority.

Organisational arrangements are complex and costly

When you first become a part of the internal workings of a local authority, it probably takes a long time — years rather than months — to understand how you fit into a very complex set of arrangements. If you have ever been involved, however marginally, in the appointment of a new person to an existing job in a local authority, did it not strike you very forcibly that, even if the job's requirements and details were very clearly stated, the new person would do it very differently from the previous job holder or from any of the other candidates, even if they all had the same basic qualifications and experience?

A description of the job will tell you why the job exists. It answers the question 'Why does the council need another person's efforts to add to all the others there?' A description of the job holder will answer the question 'What contribution is this person making, or likely to make?'

Both questions are important and need to be asked frequently and repeatedly about every single job and every single person if the people in the organisation are to help the council achieve its purposes and so give an acceptable return on the costs of using them. As we shall see, many of the most important jobs are held by councillors but, of course, the great majority are held by paid employees at considerable direct cost. This cost includes not just salary, but overheads like accommodation, supplies, communications, superannuation contributions etc., which can add almost as much again as the basic salary. One authority has a broadly applicable formula which divides salary, plus 65% for overheads, by the number of working days (226) in the year, and encourages each employee to evaluate on that basis the daily return provided for the council on its investment. The jobs undertaken for the council by councillors also involve cost to the council. No job should exist which fails to add net value to the council's work.

Not only are the two questions about the individual job and job holder important, but if the overriding purposes for which the organisation exists are to be adequately served we must also ask how each job and job holder relate to other jobs and job holders, both individually and as parts of groupings of jobs and job holders. How does the Group Accountant (Education) in the Treasurer's Department relate to the Finance Officer in the Education Department, both in terms of the formal responsibilities of the two jobs and in terms of their personal co-operation? How does the Social Services Committee relate to the Property Committee or, even more difficult, how does the Social Services Department relate to the various professional departments that deal with property matters, in terms of compatible functions and of a shared understanding between all concerned of the council's overall sense of direction?

The answers to these three questions:

▽ 'Why does the council need this job?'
▽ 'What contribution does this job holder make?'
▽ 'How do jobs and job holders inter-relate with other jobs and job holders?'

will make much more powerful statements about what in practice is much more important and central to the life of the organisation than the most passionate speech or the most carefully worded council resolution. The answers will show what the organisation is supposed to be doing and what it is actually achieving. If neither bears much relationship to the wishes of the council, then it is not in control of its organisation.

Some definitions

We have already begun to use several words which will be of continuing importance, so it will be well to be clear about their meaning. By 'the council' we mean that part of the local authority's organisation in which the formal, collective activity of all the elected representatives of the local community is focused and which is ultimately responsible for everything that the organisation does, or fails to do.

By 'the organisation' we mean all that a particular council has created in the past to give itself power, influence and impact — its libraries, its rate-collectors, its political groups, its research capability etc. The organisation is the creature of the council, but it may — or may not — be wholly under its control in practice.

By 'the organisational arrangements' we mean the decisions made by or on behalf of the council about how the organisation is shaped and operated, and the complex range of informal behaviour which is often a much more influential factor.

Organisational arrangements should create synergy

'Synergy' is a useful word to describe the successful working together of separate agents, so that the results from the whole are greater than the sum of the parts. Synergy is the reason for an organisation's existence: if individuals can achieve equally good results on their own there is no need to incur the trouble and cost of a formal connection between them. So this book is really about the harnessing of the efforts of individuals working as part of the council's organisation, to achieve the results the council intends, acting on behalf of all the individual local inhabitants. The council itself should be a means of creating synergy through its direction of communal resources. The organisation for which the council is responsible should create synergy in pursuit of those decisions. The cyclical nature of the good management thinking needed to achieve this is well known and easily stated. You must know where you are and where you are supposed to get to. You must plan the use of the available resources you will need and monitor their use in practice. You must measure what progress has been made towards the set objectives and thus understand where you are. Organisational arrangements are no exception to this treatment if synergy is to be maintained and kept pointed in the direction of the council's will. They, too, must be subjected to a process of management as rigorous and continuous as that applied to any other part of the council's activities.

Organisational complexity is likely to defeat synergy

The organisation which the council has created or inherited will be very complex, and probably the largest in the local community. Its employees may be numbered in tens of thousands, so the three basic questions:

▽ 'Why does the council need this job?'
▽ 'What contribution does this job holder make?'
▽ 'How does this job and job holder inter-relate with other jobs and job holders?'

cannot be pointed by the council (as a collective of councillors) at every job, person or grouping of jobs and persons without overwhelming the councillors who, in any event, are having to cope with sorting out the pressures from the even larger external collective of the local inhabitants.

Valid short cuts must therefore be sought to husband time, if the health of the organisation is to be constantly promoted. This requires relevant information, careful preparation and planning, adequate resources and committed consistency in implementation — as with any other important task. Such requirements need a generous allocation of time, so the book throughout encourages people to be aware of their use of time and to discipline themselves to concentrate only on what is basically important, rather than on what is merely traditional, or more tempting because it is easier, or more obvious, or is of secondary importance. Random incursions into marginal organisational change are unlikely to achieve more than very limited improvements and will overlook the substantial opportunities for improvement that ought to be taken elsewhere in the organisation, especially where the people making the decisions about the organisation ought themselves to be affected by some changes!

Reshaping the organisation must be based on an understanding of available options

The basis of organisational reshaping involves:

▽   a shared understanding of the potential flexibility of the existing organisation, and how it might be reshaped;
▽   the capacity of the existing organisation to make and implement decisions;
▽   the application of some basic techniques which are already proving their worth in local authorities and other complex organisations.

Galileo's improved telescope and the courage of his convictions radically altered contemporary understanding of the solar system, leading to practical consequences of great importance. We hope that the concepts represented by the fairly simple starting points for discussion contained in each chapter will encourage adventure in the creation of better arrangements for the more local, but nonetheless important, world of complex organisations, and of local authorities in particular, by opening up the subject to the councillors and senior employees who share responsibility for the council's work.

A shared understanding of potential flexibility

A shared understanding of potential flexibility is very important in collective decision-making. Most people in an organisation have ideas of what they individually could achieve with a magic wand! Given the collective nature of a council's decision-making and the complex inter-relationships of the various political, departmental, geographical, professional, historical, national and local groups involved in service provision, dictatorial attempts to change the organisation are unlikely to succeed. At the very least there must be broad agreement sufficient to ensure political stability and operational validity, if the sheer cost of change is to be worth while. The shared understanding of the potential for organisational changes can be stimulated by books (such as the series of which this is a part), by discussion at conferences and seminars, and by examining experiences and results in pioneering authorities and other complex organisations.

The capacity to implement decisions

However interesting the theoretical possibilites for change are as abstractions, their real value lies only in putting them into practice — and changes have to be achieved by means of, or despite, the inadequacies of the organisation which itself needs improvement! Where the inadequacies result directly from the people and the arrangements in the upper reaches of the political and bureaucratic hierarchies, it may not be possible to achieve even widely supported changes based on successful experience elsewhere. Even with adequate leadership, an external adviser, whether on secondment from another organisation or as a consultant, may be needed to supplement the capacity of the existing organisation and free it from the constraints of unthinking tradition or the obstacles to synergy which it is hoped to remove. The rather self-enclosed little world of an individual local authority in which organisational arrangements have been a neglected topic will almost always benefit from an external catalyst with a good record of achievement.

The application of proven techniques

Some local authorities have found great value in adapting to their own needs the methods pioneered and established in the arrangements of good commercial and industrial organisations. They, too, have to take organisational health seriously and, once the barriers artificially caused by separate development and specialist jargon have been overcome, much of the distinctiveness commonly associated with a local authority's work is found to be illusory or self-imposed. The experiences of local authorities struggling with complex organisational problems, and necessarily having to articulate the solutions very openly, merit wider interest from people in other complex local organisations than is usually shown, even by the local businesses affected by the local authority's activities. But lack of tools, or of potential assistance, is not usually the real reason for failing to tackle organisational problems. Lack of determination is much more common.

Questions

▲ *1. Which local issues are being emphasised by your council, formally or otherwise? What is the operational strategy for achieving practical and defined results in relation to one of these concerns?*

▲ *2. Four messages are set out on page 6. Do you agree with them? What actions should follow from your answers?*

▲ *3. Did you work through Checklist One on pages 118–119, as suggested on page 6? If not, try to do it now.*

2 Understanding the organisation

The broad outline of the formal organisation will probably be clear, because it is determined by the law or by open council decisions. It can only be altered by the same process as established it, and usually against substantial resistance. The organisational arrangements include not only the structures and jobs, formal and informal, but also the processes which bind structures and jobs together. Understanding the informal arrangements means coping with how people actually behave! One particularly important part of the arrangements is the link between the politicians and the professional staff. Another is the link with the local community, for which the council exists.

Organisational arrangements both empower and limit the power of people to act on behalf of the council

In Chapter 1 we explored the basic purposes of a democratically elected local authority and the need to determine and implement a genuine *local political agenda*. But a local authority is an artificial concept, unless and until its existence is realised in the people who are authorised to carry out various tasks. This artificiality has two sources. First, there are laws enacted by Parliament which create, and limit, the powers of the council. Secondly, there are the arrangements made by the council within those powers, which authorise and limit the powers of people to act on behalf of the council — whether in committees or as employees.

The formal organisation of a local authority is the most open there can be, since the legislative provisions are public and all decisions made by the council must normally result from publicly accessible processes. The openness of organisation means that the formal decision-making structure and processes of a local authority have to be defined very precisely, with any alterations being subjected to the same formal processes as those by which they were created. Unless, therefore, a council has a constant process for reviewing and renewing the continued effectiveness and efficiency of its own organisation in relation to changing needs, and a determined strategy for assuring and maintaining its continuing relevance and health, the result will usually be a seemingly permanent formal organisation which continues to shape and limit the efforts of councillors and employees alike, despite any changes in the needs of the local community they are there to serve.

The case for constant attention being paid to organisational arrangements is very powerful, yet it is rare for a council to practise systematic and co-ordinated organisational review. We need to remember the strong forces always at work to protect the *status quo* which formality tends to encourage even when change is desirable. Some of these forces will be examined in detail as we progress through the book but the three principal reasons for not assuming continued organisational relevance lightly may be summarised as:

▽   organisational inertia;
▽   complexity; and
▽   competing current pressures for internal supremacy.

Organisational inertia

What often begins as a proper political concern for achieving results 'at the sharp end', rather than wasting time on 'internal' matters, can soon degenerate into the disruption of the internal organisational games played within the immediate village community of the town or county hall, the divisional offices or the individual school. The cumulative effect of maintaining pecking orders and promotion ladders, of keeping the trade unions quiet or influential councillors happy, of coping with a never-ending succession of public demands for more and better services despite limited finances, of fighting the political PR battle with an eye on the next local or general elections, is very powerful. It tends to push the need for internal organisational improvement into the background. Only a local crisis or a superior instruction forces the need for change. But a local authority, as we have seen, does not exist primarily to provide a good career for employees, nor as a satisfying activity for councillors. The council's *local political agenda* should be more than a trial of strength between national political parties, or a begging bowl for resources, or a complaints service for the public. The diversion of effort that internalised politics takes from the council's basic purposes of political pluralism, democratic participation and sensitive, relevant, service delivery leads inexorably to organisational inertia.

Complexity

The sheer size and scale of even the smallest local authorities' activities and responsibilities often frightens people from tackling a review of current arrangements. The need to comply with increasingly complex legal requirements, the detail of the council's own inherited arrangements, the sheer size of the employee numbers and resources involved in current operations, the interaction of one decision with another, the remoteness in practice of the council itself from actual service delivery, the inappropriate highlighting of detail, on the pretext of democracy, all these features of a local authority make for complexity which is daunting, and again discourage purposeful control of organisational arrangements. The temptation to dabble in minor detail, instead of working at the complexity of the problems confronting our level of responsibility, must be resisted.

Internal competition

But the third reason why the organisational arrangements stay the same is one which so often gets in the way of any beneficial change. People can agree that there ought to be change, can agree the broadest of *directions* in which change should take place, but cannot agree the detail of the change or how to break into it in practice, so stalemate is reached and the *status quo* is maintained. Some of the argument about detail will arise because the group of people involved are making decisions about consequential details inappropriate to their level of responsibility. We all have our individual preferred ways of doing things, but it is unhelpful to try to force others to carry out their responsibilities as though we were in their position.

Where the decision-making is appropriate, the mixture of individual perceptions which the people involved bring to bear must, of course, be taken seriously but their individual reasons, or even ideals, can rarely be taken as the simple absolutes they are often asserted to be. 'Open government', for example, is an important principle which has always applied to the decision-making processes of the full council meeting, and it is logical that it should now apply to decision-making by committees acting under delegated powers from the council. But its blanket application to every official action by a councillor, e.g. in making a complaint, or pursuing an individual enquiry, or meeting in a party group, would lead to absurdity. Provision has to be made somewhere for exploration of issues without the glare of publicity and its consequences, otherwise the council's decision-making will be dominated by prejudice. So a balance has to be struck between the competing ideals of open accountability and thorough exploration of complex issues. The nature of the balance which should be struck will be influenced by the stand-point of the individual leader, chairman, 'opposition' councillor, divisional surveyor, news reporter etc. involved in considering the arrangements. Since the normal ethos of a council is collective decision-making, in which a decision is reached despite inevitable differences of opinion, the task of keeping the organisation healthy requires its own agreed processes for reaching workable decisions in just the same way that the council reaches other controversial decisions to achieve its purposes. Ad hoc responses to individual organisational challenges as they arise are inadequate. Deletion of redundant arrangements and the maintenance of overall cohesion require committed decisions, careful planning and consistent action.

What are organisational arrangements? Structures, jobs and processes

What are organisational arrangements? It is difficult to say at first! So this chapter is about understanding the organisation, and especially how the operational machine relates to people, so that it can be shaped and reshaped to help them give of their best towards achieving the council's purposes. First we look at the different components of the machine and then consider how to evaluate their usefulness. The ultimate aim is to produce a machine which empowers individual people to act on the council's behalf in achieving what it is in business to do, within limits which prevent confusion and abuse of power.

In a local authority the identification of its component committees and departments is fairly easy — at least as far as their names and broad purposes go. If you become directly involved you will, in addition, have met or heard about certain people — the chairman of the education committee or the chief environmental health officer, for example — and you can make a reasonable guess about their roles and significance. In pursuing your particular interests, you will be aware of certain sub-committees, certain working relationships and certain key people. From dealing with practical problems you will know who is responsible, for example, for street repairs, but what else that person deals with, and who else is involved with decisions about street repairs, may not be at all clear or relevant to the individual problems. And if it comes to pinning down responsibility for something important which has gone wrong or needs to be done, it is almost impossible to get behind organisational clichés about 'the overall responsibility of the Chief

Officer' or the committee, even though the personal connection is obviously very distant. A determined inquiry into how a decision came to be made will usually reveal a bewildering set of interactions involving a complex pattern of political, operational, professional and personal structures, processes and reasons, many of which will not be concerned solely, or even mainly, with the point at issue. Organisational arrangement are not only complex; they are often obscure.

Yet organisation is only a means to an end, capable of being changed openly by those in charge and, in more subtle ways, by people's behaviour. In examining the council's operational machine in a way which gets behind superficial appearances and takes note of how people are actually working together, we need to be aware not only of the machine which the council has formally authorised or inherited, but also of the informal assumptions and practices which so frequently supplement, or even negate, the formal machinery. Only when what is actually happening is understood can we be satisfied that all is well, or hope to change things for the better with confidence.

It is obvious that simple collecting together all we happen to know about the organisation will rarely help us to achieve a coherent, total understanding. The detail will overwhelm us. What we need are the key features relevant to our own level of responsibility so that we can manage the inter-relationships with the people to whom, or for whom, we are directly accountable. These key features will, at each level, shape the more detailed parts of the machine within the framework they establish, just as our decisions have to fit within the framework we have been given by Parliament, or by the council or by another intermediate level of authority. Each level and each section of the organisation constitutes a complex community for its participants. The most we can hope to do successfully in detail is to achieve coherence for our own responsibilities. The more senior the level, the greater the need to concentrate on key controls.

In a small-scale, locally contained organisation, whose people are all directly affected by the success or failure of their joint efforts, the basic operational machine can be very simple and easy to vary successfully. But as the organisation becomes larger and more complex, it increasingly separates into specialists who are often not directly concerned about the end results. Increasingly it is governed by its own traditions. The result is inflexibility and lack of purposeful co-operation. The coming together of people to make the kind of impact on external circumstances which is the reason for the organisation's existence, and which is greater than could be achieved by people sectionally or individually, gives way to internalised priorities of status quite divorced from the need to achieve success for the organisation as a whole. Organisational effectiveness — the achievement of collective synergy to tackle difficult challenges — needs a machine constructed from:

▽   clear structures;
▽   of inter-related jobs; based on
▽   sound processes which enable plans to be made, resources to be deployed, integration of effort to be achieved, and collective control to be applied.

The structures determine how well the jobs fit together, and the processes provide the linkages between them. The education committee is one peg of the council's committee structure; being a member of the education committee is a job; reaching a decision in the committee involves several processes. The school meals section is one peg of the education department's structure; being a school meals assistant is a job; working with others to produce a school meal involves several processes.

The obvious starting point is to identify the formal arrangements clearly

The formal organisational arrangements are partly fixed by law, but are mainly decided by or on behalf of the council to show what it (at the time it made the decisions) expected of the people appointed to the jobs involved. In contrast to the formal arrangements are the informal, arising from the way people behave in relation to each other. Sometimes they are so well established that they appear to be formal. By law, a chairman of the council must be appointed by the council; by decision of the council, powers are delegated to committees — formally. By convention, members often work together in party political groups but alleviate the divisiveness this can cause by creating individual relationships — informally.

The local authority itself is clearly a creation of the law, important facets being the size of the council and its range of powers and duties. By law, certain committees have to be formed and certain processes followed in reaching and recording the council's decisions. Obviously the very artificiality of a local authority's existence requires attention to legal advice when variations in its arrangements are being considered but, in practice, the council is fairly free to determine its own operational machine, including the important power to delegate to committees, sub-committees or employees.

Formal structures

The formal structural arrangements made by the council may well be scattered through volumes of minutes recording all the decisions made by the council, its committees and sub-committees. Those formal structural arrangements made by employees under delegated powers will be even more difficult to gather together, but the basic formal structure consisting of the powers and duties of each committee and sub-committee and the existence of several departments, each with a determined formal hierarchy of top jobs, will easily be set down, and is usually done so in the council's year book. An up-to-date departmental organisation chart, showing at least the levels of intermediate command, and a description of the broad nature of the work done by each section, ought also to be available, to help 'outsiders' find their way about and 'insiders' to keep control. Unfortunately, this information is thought to be so obvious by the 'insiders' that it is often not adequately recorded and others have to rely on chance contacts or persistent enquiries to reach the people they need.

The overall formal structures — the 'family trees' of the department — are therefore readily capable of being defined. But how clearly is it possible to define the individual jobs within the structure, or how they relate to each other?

Formal jobs

It is now quite common for a job description to be a part of a contract of employment for a senior post, usually consisting of a list of formal duties with a catch-all clause at the end. From such job descriptions as are available, we may learn what the council at one time expected the job holders to do, but probably not much about what the job holders were expected to achieve. Many jobs will not have any kind of up-to-date detailed description available — not even an out-of-date one! Few councils set out the results they expect someone appointed to the chair of a committee to achieve, or someone appointed to one of the many employee jobs which actually deliver a council service to a client. It is a mixture of tradition and individual initiative which usually determines the substance of most jobs. They are rarely tied explicitly to the council's current intentions.

Formal processes

The formal processes will have their current shape determined by a scatter of previous decisions, as well as by the law. A council will govern many processes through its standing orders and financial regulations, e.g. the order and maximum length of speeches in a council debate, or what a committee must do to obtain a supplementary estimate, and the law will require items affecting education, police or social services functions normally to be considered in the relevant committee before determination by the council. Ad hoc amendments over the years will have dealt with some current organisational problems but a comprehensive review of what is needed to bind together all the formal components of the council's machine is likely to reveal gaps and irrelevances. In one council an instruction to present a progress report to the monthly council meeting on the number of council houses completed was followed without question for many years after the crisis which prompted the instruction had passed. Few councils have a rigorous process for planning and managing their formal agendas. They are usually little more than ad hoc responses to operational needs.

The formal structures, jobs and processes are abstractions often drawn in diagrams or described in writing. One would think they could be easily varied as required, simply by altering the diagram or amending a paragraph. So long as they remain abstractions, this is the case; but once the jobs are filled, the status of each individual person within the community created by the organisation is determined by the formal structures, jobs and processes. A job title, one's ranking in the organisation chart, membership of a particular grouping, or involvements in particular processes convey important messages — important for the individual and for those who deal with the individual. The messages cannot be lightly changed. In local authorities where there is no active management of performance with a view to achieving council-determined results, the formal abstractions become powerful status symbols and increase the focus of attention on internal rather than external impact.

The informal arrangements reflect people's behaviour

By contrast with the formal, the informal structures, jobs and processes of the organisation reflect the actual behaviour of the individuals who are appointed to the formal jobs. Mr Smith is more approachable than Mrs Green, so anyone with the freedom to choose brings problems for Mr Smith to solve, even if Mrs Green's formal job indicates that she would be more appropriate. Councillor Jones is known to be specially concerned about social services, so the councillor's informal support for a proposal is sought by pointing out the particular benefit to social services, even when that may not be the only point of the proposal! A senior officer may have a poor reputation for competence, so councillors and colleagues alike informally by-pass that job holder whenever possible. The office cleaner expects to find your office available for its 'weekly do' at 5.45pm each Thursday, so you find an alternative location whenever necessary. Councillor White is known as a gossip, so if you want something spread around you tell him 'in confidence'!

Not all these informal arrangements are important and some are ephemeral; but some will have a profound effect on the way people actually work together, whatever the formal arrangements may expect of them. The structural line of command will be distorted by the regular by-passing of incompetence, as will the shape of the jobs carried out by the incompetent and by those who substitute their work to compensate. Formal processes can be supplemented, or even drained of real value, by the informal relationships of those who 'get on well together'. Does the council wish to accept these informal components, or to vary them?

Because the council is a decision-making collective, without whose authority nothing can be done on the council's behalf, it is inevitable that informal power-blocs will be created as individuals seek to convert their private agenda into council decisions. A political party group is an obvious example; a close and effective partnership between a committee chairman and a chief officer is another. Within a department a common professional background may bind people together in a supportive 'old boy network'. Between departments there can be a seemingly unbridgeable chasm because the separated parts of the formal structure each evoke an exclusive loyalty from the people whose work is focused inwards, producing rivalry and competition for the council's favour. One organisation, not a local authority, which extensively decentralised its work now has to employ security guards to prevent one section gaining ground by raiding the materials allocated to another!

Conventional informality

Some of the informal components of the operational machine are more obvious than others. They are so well established that their impact and seeming permanence clouds their difference from the truly formal — that which is unalterable except in the way in which it was created, by authority of the law or by authority of the council. But these conventional informal components, even though they may include some of the most powerful influences on the way people collaborate, can be disregarded by those involved, should they so choose. They are, therefore, not directly controllable by the council unless they are transferred from the informal to the formal organisation.

The most obvious conventional organisation will be the party political groups. These affect the working relationships between councillors of the same group, and between those of different groups, with employees, with the press, with pressure groups and with the national and local organisations of the political parties. They have their own structures, jobs and processes. It would be unreal to define the organisational arrangements of most councils without reference to the conventions of party politics.

Sometimes these conventions are written down, e.g. an agreement about which political group shall nominate the next mayor. At some point a decision has to be made whether to make a convention formal. Thus, the leadership of the council may have to be recognised as a formal job if standing orders are to give the job holder special privileges or responsibilities in formal debate.

In the employee components, too, there are many informal variations or supplements to the formal which are sufficiently well established to be regarded as conventions. As the narrow limitations of the formal departmental system are increasingly challenged by new problems which do not neatly fit into the departmental framework, the more strongly motivated people link their work together across the formal structures to produce more relevant results. These informal arrangements, e.g. a meeting of senior officers co-ordinating the planning of service development proposals, can often indicate the way in which the formal components should be reshaped.

Political/operational links

Perhaps the most striking informal modification of the formal machinery is the way in which councillor/employee relationships have had to be managed to cope with party political divisions within the council. In theory, the council is an executive body acting on behalf of the local inhabitants, and each councillor has an equal right to participate in the decisions being taken because each has one vote. Items coming before the council for decision are supported by official information and advice, and a majority of those present and voting decides what to do. There is no separation, as in the Westminster/Whitehall model, between Parliament and executive government. Specific parliamentary approval is not a prerequisite for ministerial executive action. By contrast, in a local authority, action can only be taken on the direct or clearly delegated authority of the council. The leader of the majority political party is not a local equivalent of the Prime Minister, and the 'opposition' is entitled to information from the council's organisation on equal terms with the party in control.

The consequence for the Council's senior advisers and managers is that although they are employed by the council and are accountable to it, unlike a civil servant who is answerable to the minister, they increasingly have to accommodate to a Whitehall/Westminster type of pattern. As national politics have increasingly dominated conventional arrangements in local authorities, the national model for political leadership and the implementation of one party's ideas has been increasingly adopted. The chairman of the council is superseded by the leader as the prime mover of policy issues; the chairman of a committee becomes a local minister in the eyes of the public because, informally, a majority of councillors accord this status within their party group and can be relied upon to back the initiatives of the informal political job holders by a formal vote on behalf of the council. Those members not in the majority group are effectively confined to the 'opposition' functions of criticism and exposure. How do the employees fulfil their duties to the council as a whole, while recognising the political dynamics of reality?

The answer varies from one authority to another. At one extreme the processes for collaboration between the informal job holders in the informal member structure and the formal job holders in the formal employee structure may be minimal because the party politics are kept well behind the formal facade of the committee structure and processes. The councillors and employees are still uncertain of the propriety or the power of the party discipline, relying on the provision in the 'Purple Book'[5] that 'the officer should not be called upon to advise any political group of the employing authority either as to the work of the group or as to the work of the authority, neither shall he be required to attend any meeting of any political group'.

At the other extreme, a similar result is achieved because the party discipline can be so dominant that the formal job holders are excluded from influencing political decisions, and alternative sources of expertise and advice are found. In between these two extremes, a variety of informal processes operate — officer advice available to a party group meeting, or to a 'chairman's cabinet', on clearly laid down terms; close liaison between the senior employees of a department and councillors specially chosen by the party groups to discuss relevant policy options and progress in their implementation; employees, of known party political sympathies or not, appointed specifically to provide links between the political and the departmental arrangements. As more councils have become 'hung' (i.e. no one political group has an overall majority) conventions to deal with the mismatch between the formal unity of the council, as employer and sole source of authority, and the reality of its acute political disunity have had to be consciously invented to replace those which had often grown up over many years of evolution under very different political dynamics.

The interaction of the informal with the formal organisational arrangements determines whether or not the latter can be regarded as satisfactory. It is always worth examining this interaction most closely before embarking on any formal restructuring.

Don't forget the importance of arrangements for external links

So far we have concentrated almost entirely on the application of structures, jobs and processes to the people involved within the council's operational machine, but external arrangements are also important if the council is to relate effectively to the local community. Despite the wide representative duties which take up so much time for councillors, there is increasing concern that local authorities should improve their relationship with the public, whether as clients of the council's services, as local taxpayers, or as electors involved in the fulfilment of the council's political purposes. Each local authority also has the possibility of extending its influence and creating additional synergy in pursuance of its purposes by linking with other public authorities and public-spirited private bodies active within the local community.

As with the internal arrangements, there will be formal and informal external structures, jobs and processes which will determine the impact the council makes. The council's involvement in national arrangements, such as a National Joint Council for Salaries and Conditions of Service of Employees, will formally replace the structure, jobs and processes with which it would otherwise have to provide itself to make the equivalent decisions. When services are decentralised, extra structures, formal and informal, will probably be needed to make the more local sensitivity mean something which will work in practice. The practical requirements of the media will lead to jobs and processes being established for operational and political publicity purposes. Processes for identifying public concerns and evaluating the weight of pressure groups will constantly be developing. Simply because 'the public' has so many forms and voices, there is a constant need to check the relevance of current structures, jobs and processes for 'external affairs'.

Questions

▲   1. *Identify an organisational weakness in your organisation. Why has it not been changed? Analyse the forces that maintain the weakness.*

▲   2. *Just how important do you think the formal structures are, compared with the informal ways in which things are decided?*

▲   3. *Take the local issue which you identified when dealing with Question 1 of Chapter 1 on page 14. Identify other organisations that might contribute to a solution. What further arrangements could the council make with these organisations to improve their contribution?*

3 Using the organisation

In setting about the reshaping of the organisation, concentrate on the area you can influence and examine it in detail. Take delegation seriously and keep formality to the necessary minimum so that flexibility can flourish. The criterion for organisational development is 'What will help the council to fulfil its purposes?', i.e. the fundamental purposes of local, democratic government — about which there should be widespread agreement. A sound organisation needs a robust, agreed base for action, including a defined process for handling disagreements. Inherited, passively accepted organisation will rarely meet current needs, but the key to success lies in having relevant processes which the people involved are prepared to accept, rather than in imposed formal restructuring.

After analysis — modification

Having identified the three components of the operational machine which the council has created or (more likely) inherited — the structures, the jobs and the processes, in their formal and their informal guises — we now consider how to modify the organisation so that it more relevantly promotes the council's purposes. In effect, harnessing people to the organisation empowers them to act on behalf of the council, but within limits. The sole reason for having an organisation is to promote the council's decisions, and what those decisions are is the subject of the next chapter. The abstract organisation takes effect through the skills, energies and commitment of the people involved and the way they are directed to act constructively together. If people were empowered to act without any limitation on their freedom the results, however well intentioned, would be chaotic. Inevitably, because all legal and political authority is centralised in the council, its supportive and implementational arrangements will be bureaucratic, authority 'cascading' down from the source and covering an ever wider range of actions but, with each lower level of delegated power, becoming more specific in its scope.

The result of a determined reshaping should be a more controllable organisation whose formal definition states what the council expects of the many people involved and enables them to direct their creativity, enterprise and commitment in pursuit of the council's decisions.

Stage 1. Be clear, and don't get sucked into secondary detail

The first stage for considering the merits of the existing organisational arrangements is obviously to be clear about what they are. Unless there is an adequate diagram or description sufficiently detailed to give a common understanding of what is actually going on, both to those who will reshape and to those whose work will be reshaped, the risk of unintended and undesirable consequences is very high. Simply altering the formal structure at a senior level without considering the other components will rarely achieve advantageous change, and the cost in terms of morale, motivation and achievement, as well as in financial compensation, may well be high.

Although the formal structures and jobs at the most senior levels will be readily identifiable, what happens, formally or informally, below that level will be increasingly difficult to determine. From the council's vantage point, the detail becomes too fine to be comprehended, though in practice that is often no deterrent to decisions about ad hoc detailed changes being made at this remote level! We will be considering the art of delegation in the next chapter, but the principles apply equally to organisational development as to other aspects of the organisation. Each level of management, including the council and its committees, should be clear about the organisational arrangements within its own span of control and be satisfied that they serve the council's purposes. Consequential arrangements can then be left to those accountable for them, subject to the controls which we discuss in Chapter 6. The clarity and quality of successive levels in the organisation will therefore reflect the clarity and quality of superior line management, and in many local authorities that may not be well developed. In one local authority, a job analysis exercise involving all the 'principal officers', i.e. the senior middle managers, included the instruction: 'Describe your job in relation to its superiors and its subordinates.'

Although that authority had already developed its managerial capacity to a reasonable standard, the lack of correspondence between different people's answers, and the number of employees who couldn't give a clear answer, indicated a disquietingly hazy formal structure of jobs at that important level. The same job analysis exercise provided a basis for the jobs, once clearly structured and defined, to be individually evaluated for salary grading by a panel of more senior managers drawn from other departments than the one from time to time under consideration. Two benefits ensued to the council: first, the introverted ideas of relative importance within each department were subjected to a healthy critique which exposed many further weaknesses; secondly, the exposure of the formal structure to colleagues from other departments began to widen understanding of who did what, resulting in a reduction of duplication and an increase in synergy. Clarity of formal arrangements doesn't just happen; organisational fitness for purpose doesn't just happen; synergy from co-operation doesn't just happen. These things have to be organised with care and determination, based on clarity.

The informal arrangements are even more difficult to describe with clarity than the formal, apart from the well-established conventions. Discussion to get the 'feel' of things is often the best way to gain understanding, rather than always striving to reduce everything to a precise diagram or written report. Shared subjective judgment will illuminate why one group of people seem not to 'get on' with another, or how far the informal processes contradict the formal. Because the informal components are the result of people's behaviour, great sensitivity is required from the outset if those same people are to be motivated to work together better.

Stage 2. What should be formal? As little as possible!

Having clearly established what is the purpose and the existing shape of the organisation for which we are responsible, we need to consider carefully what the council should formally determine and what should be left to varying degrees of informality. The council needs to confer adequate authority and to impose some clear limits on the people appointed to work on its behalf — the formalities; but those people need maximum freedom and minimum hindrance if they are to use their personal skills, experience and commitment to optimum effect — the informal. The extent of formal delegation must therefore be considered. A council which is satisfied, for example, that the formal processes it has approved for job grading are adequately monitored and related to financial and other decisions need not formally approve the detail of other than the most senior jobs and structures which result. Clear purposes against which to measure results, and adequate delegation of consequential detail, remove many of the control needs which are otherwise needed. But some formality is certainly necessary.

The first justification for formality is propriety — a key virtue in a local authority and one for which the record is very good in Britain. Because the authority is an artificial legal person, its decisions have to be formally taken within statutory powers and recorded in accordance with the law. Every action taken and every penny of expenditure incurred on its behalf must be properly authorised, directly or indirectly, by the council. Its propriety is subject to the oversight of the courts, inspectors, the external auditor and the 'Ombudsman'. The consequence is an enormous emphasis on the observance of legalities and the precise recording of decisions taken. If this degree of formality is attached to detail, including therefore any changes in detail, excessive formality is the inevitable result. If, however, key discussions by the council are implemented by people with delegated powers, less formality is required as the consequences are progressively delegated to subordinates for determination under the umbrella of the wider formality of the senior-level decisions.

A second justification for formality is that it conveys important messages about the council's priorities to employees and to those who deal with the organisation. A council which enforces clear major lines of formal accountability will create a very different working atmosphere from one which allows responsibility for results to be lost in a general morass of confused inter-relationships. A council which creates formal processes for establishing to what it will commit itself beyond the horizon of the next financial year will find it easier to convince employees, contractors, pressure groups and other public authorities how far it means business. The greater the recorded commitment, and the fewer the messages, the more powerful they become. The relevance of formal structures and processes is more important than their quantity.

Formality, by definition, lacks flexibility and a local authority needs some formality to give shape to its existence. A job's formal title and formal place in a structure confers status and creates group loyalties. Changes in these formalities will therefore usually be achieved only at the cost of considerable opposition and disruption, from people who may have to be bought off at considerable expense. Whether the county archivist should be transferred from the county secretary's to the county librarian's department, whether two professionally based departments should be merged to form a property department, or whether there should be a separate libraries committee, are all propositions likely to create major internal battles for status-conscious people. Whether a job should be called 'Director of Education' or 'Chief Education Officer' can produce hours of highly principled debate on the messages that the different titles are perceived to give. Unless the changes will clearly create a significant advantage in achieving the council's purposes, they are not worth the effort involved. The consequence of this typical rigidity, however, is that the formal arrangements will rarely reflect the latest dynamics of the council's decisions about what it wants to achieve. This underlines the need to keep formalities to very broadly agreed arrangements and leave the consequential details open to more flexible informality.

A few years ago, a local authority pursued informally the possibility of job descriptions for some of the jobs to which members were appointed by the council. Just what did the council expect of the chairman of the council, or of a committee, or of the leader of the council or of the leader of the opposition? It was realised that, although everyone involved in and with the jobs thought the duties were 'obvious', what was obvious to one person was not obvious to others. Thus there was no agreed basis for considering suitability, or for giving guidance to newly appointed councillor job holders and to the employees who supported their work. Draft job descriptions were drawn up and subjected to informed discussion by councillors and then more formally in the sub-committee dealing with the task. The council's formal decision was wisely and deliberately confined to 'noting' the final versions and, when changed political control made some parts of the descriptions inappropriate, it was readily possible to identify what should remain, what should be amended and what should be left for experimental development. If the council had 'approved' the descriptions, it would have extended formality beyond what was necessary and created a need to observe a very difficult formal process to obtain amendments. In Chapter 10 we propose detailed job descriptions for councillors but, again, more in the spirit of focusing thought and behaviour than for formal adoption.

The virtue of flexibility which the informal arrangements enjoy does not necessarily mean a loss of clarity. As we have seen, the well-established conventional components can be recorded with complete clarity but without rigidity, like the job descriptions just referred to. The distinction between what should be formal and what should be informal is important in ensuring that the council controls only what it thinks it is important to control formally, leaving to the initiatives of well-motivated job holders the development of relevant, informal structures, jobs and processes which are clarified, amended and reviewed in the normal management processes.

Stage 3. Are the components which you control, or influence, helpful to the council's purposes?

Having established the way the existing machine works, with sufficient clarity to understand the need for changes, we come to the criteria by which we can judge what to change and what to keep, what to make formal and what to make or leave informal. Throughout this chapter we have used the phrase 'the Council's decisions' to indicate the council's direction of the organisation, and in the next chapter we will look in more detail at how a council determines and sets out what those *directions* are. For the moment we will assume that the council follows the standard cyclical process of setting out what it intends to achieve, of providing the resources needed to gain those achievements, of measuring the results actually achieved and readjusting accordingly. It is, of course, a big assumption. The important point for present purposes is that 'providing the resources needed' includes shaping and reshaping the organisational arrangements so as to enable the resource of the council's people to work together with maximum freedom, but minimum discord and irrelevance. The council's most important resource is its people, and they need organising if they are to work together to optimum effect.

Bearing in mind that our purpose in shaping the arrangements is to enable synergy to flow from co-operation, the components we are dealing with are not in themselves 'good' or 'bad', so much as 'helpful' or 'unhelpful' to the achievement of the council's purposes. The likelihood is that, in the absence of adequate direction from the council, any collection of individuals with differing backgrounds, skills, ambitions and tasks will have developed private agendas and loyalties which are tangential, or even counter, to the purposes for which the council has brought them together.

The task of starting to evaluate the existing arrangements from scratch is going to be a formidable one because it is necessary to use the mechanisms of the existing defective arrangements and thus arouse the suspicions of many vested interests. The temptation will be to continue to adapt the informal and to add on new formal arrangements, rather than go against the existing grain. In this way the waste caused by inefficient and irrelevant bureaucracy increases, until a crisis is reached. This can then result in sudden and insensitive change, causing great disruption and often ignoring the need for purposeful changes at more senior levels. Practical advice on how to get started is given in Chapter 11, but the aim should be to make the continuous reshaping of the arrangements a part of the normal evolution of the authority. Its reputation as a worthwhile and useful local means of continuing to solve local problems is at stake.

Only if the evaluation is dominated by pursuit of the council's directions will the characteristics of narrow organisational loyalty, focused on immediate formal status, be overcome. Certainty of purpose must replace certainty of familiar structure if the great mass of routine service delivery which is often cut off from new political direction is to continue as a direct consequence of the council's current intentions. But the phrase 'the council's direction' implies a unity in the council which exists only in the artificial formality of its recorded decisions. We know that, informally, the council is likely to be divided into opposing sections simply because one of its functions is to bring into the open and then to determine local controversial issues. Before pursuing the singleminded implementation of the council's intentions, whether in the design of the organisation to be used or in the strategy for results to be followed, we must analyse the robustness of the starting point for action. How can the council be said to have 'intentions'?

A sound organisation needs a robust basis for its development

The common local authority image of constant rivalry and bickering about principles unrelated to consistency about practice, which struggles for popularity with that of the Trumpton Mayor summoning the Fire Brigade to re-set the Town Hall clock is, of course, unfair but partly justified by the way the council behaves in public. A council's procedures are designed to cope with controversy — that is why all the councillors are entitled to vote and why there is legal provision for a casting vote in the event of an equality of votes. But the formal council and committee processes are only a small part of what is done by the authority and it may be valuable to consider what processes should be provided to underline the considerable areas of substantial agreement which exist within the council about that range of activities. Those responsible to the council for the bulk of what the organisation is actually doing in the community deserve a firmer base for their work than a scatter of ancient minutes and current political silence.

There is likely to be widespread agreement about the value of local democracy and the need for processes which make it effective. There is likely to be widespread agreement about the need for effective democratic control of what is being done in the council's name. The need for processes to help councillors explore the shape of the council's formal structures, jobs and processes to fulfil the three Widdicombe attributes ought to be able to bridge the deepest divisions within a democratically concerned council. There is also likely to be agreement on the need for much of the existing service provision — reshaping the details of how it is provided ought not to be a matter for the council at all below the most important decisions, if good management is in place — yet operational managers know too well the risk of inconsistent or technically unsound detailed decisions from a remote level of higher authority at a late stage of implementation of a council decision.

If the requirements of good line management provide one reason for thinking about how the council should organise to cope consistently and clearly with internal controversy, a more selfish prompt to politicians might be the opportunity to put a clearer display of political wares in a better shop window! In recent years the pursuit of more 'open' government by local authorities has rightly forced the traditional openness of the council meeting on to the committees which increasingly exercise powers of final decision on the council's behalf. In practice, it appears to have had little effect in improving the public's understanding of the dilemmas facing the council, or the council's understanding of local opinion. Little thought is applied to whether the window was in the right place to catch the public's attention, still less whether the appropriate goods were on display. Given that in most local authorities the actual decisions are pre-determined in secret party meetings, the formal council or committee meeting is no longer an exploration of operational options, yet the agenda often remains a collection of operational issues. Why obscure the real political confrontations by finding it always embarrassing to agree across the party divides on managerial or practical questions. In any event, the validity of testing a proposition from opposing sides is diluted if every proposition is subjected to the same treatment from the same opposing sides. As the council's programme for action in its *local political agenda* becomes clearer, the need for random or blanket confrontation on any issue, as an internal end in itself, becomes reduced.

There are two principal reasons why the local political debate can degenerate even with the best of intentions. The removal of opportunities for exploration, negotiation and compromise which the committees used to fulfil when they met in private to prepare recommendations for the open council meeting is one. Adequate new processes have usually not been devised to replace comprehensively those opportunities across the range of political decision-making. The second is too narrow, unthinking political group loyalty — the political equivalent of internalised departmental loyalty. Some years ago now, when the committee clerk in the highways committee accidentally transposed the names of two roads, at the junction of which the committee was recommending the council to erect a 'Halt' sign, the committee chairman found himself in council justifying traffic being halted on the major of the two roads, because the recommendation in its mistaken form had been questioned by the local councillor, who happened to be a member of 'the opposition'. So what is surely needed in the arrangements is behind-the-scenes opportunity for adequate access to information and advice, and for exploring how far confrontation is a necessary consequence of political policies which it is important to establish in public.

Don't be prisoners of the existing arrangements. Create better ones — especially better processes

If there is a rigorous examination of the extent to which existing arrangements help the council to fulfil the three Widdicombe attributes — of political pluralism, democratic involvement and locally sensitive services — the need for improvements will usually be obvious. Why be prisoners of the existing arrangements? Why should councillors always meet formally in the same place? Why are agendas confined to a list of issues for executive decision? Why do agendas rarely provide an opportunity for the council to consider its responsibilities coherently? In times when it is customary for councillors to speak without apparent embarrassment 'on behalf of the ratepayers' or 'on behalf of the working classes', just what means are available to inform local people of current dilemmas and alternative viewpoints and how can the council find out what people actually think about them? Even if the only acceptable answer is 'the ballot box', the practical arrangements to link the electorate with the issues faced by the council deserve careful local consideration, and need special attention to sift out the operational problems of normal service provision which otherwise will clog the conduct of effective political debate.

In several authorities the council has created processes to produce better agendas — minimising time-wasting or unintended side-effects on operations, and maximising opportunities for argument on the really important issues — across the whole range of formal meetings. Perhaps now that local democratic values are so obviously under threat, from central domination and alternative forms of local government, we shall see a new enthusiasm in local authorities for assessing just how effective their democratic processes are. Democracy is, after all, their principal distinctive feature and the source of their authority.

Throughout the three stages of reshaping the organisational arrangements — by obtaining clarity, by balancing formality and informality, and by making arrangements which serve the council's purposes — most people will first be tempted to concentrate on structures and jobs. These are the parts of the machine that give or threaten individual status whether as a member of a particular committee or department, or as a job holder. By designating a job, or redesigning a structure, the council can neatly express a particular message, but unwisely ignore the consequences for other jobs and the way they operate together. Although it is from the efforts of individuals that most of a local authority's impact on the local community comes, it is the processes which link the individual parts of the machine together, and it is the processes which will determine the extent to which the machine achieves a synergy greater than the sum of its parts. The council is itself the result of an electoral process to provide a communal synergy and the ways in which it reaches all its decisions, except those which are delegated to individual employees, are also processes. Clearly, processes are very important and invite skill and thoughtfulness in their creation, maintenance and amendment. But because processes are themselves artificial, they will only work to the extent that they command the support of the people they involve. Processes should therefore normally be based on widespread agreement about their necessity and their design. Political groups may disagree about what ought to be decided, but can still agree about the appropriateness of processes needed to reach a decision. Departments and committees can be rivals in trying to obtain a greater share of available resources but can agree on the processes needed to help the council reach a decision fairly. Processes can rarely be imposed against the will of the people they involve and still achieve success.

Having analysed the existing organisation and considered the importance of its relevance to what the council is hoping to achieve in fulfilling its basic purposes, we now turn to the way the council makes key decisions which give a clear sense of direction for those within its organisation to follow.

Questions

▲ 1. *'The relevance of formal structures and processes is more important than their quantity' (page 27). Do you agree? If so, what minimum formal structures and processes do you need to help you achieve your contribution to the council's objectives? What could be cut out?*

▲ 2. *Take the same issue of concern to the council in the local community which you identified when dealing with Question 1 of Chapter 1 on page 14. To what extent is there agreement/disagreement in the council about what should be achieved, about how it should be achieved, about how soon it should be achieved? Is the council's view clearly recorded, sufficiently to give managers a sound basis for their actions?*

▲ 3. *How are the processes which link the parts of the organisation together (such as planning, resource allocation, financial control, review) kept relevant and effective? Whose job is it to check their effectiveness?*

4 An agenda for the organisation

A council should concentrate on clear operationally meaningful *directions* about targets for locally effective action, about the money it will make available to help hit their targets, and about the operating values that must be used by its agents. Such *directions* require careful processing but, once set out, they will enable the council to get rid of clutter by careful delegation, and to control the whole of its responsibilities. Detail may be interesting but it prevents real local democracy.

'Members' concern with detail leaves them too little time to take the more important decisions'

The effectiveness of local authority management was thoroughly reviewed by the Maud Committee on the *Management of Local Government* in 1967[6], and its analysis and recommendations still repay careful study. Its major conclusion was that:

> 1. Radical changes in the local government of England and Wales are needed . . . the country is not getting full value in terms of human happiness . . .
> 3. First, it is due to the survival, in the great majority of local authorities, both large and small, of a nineteenth century tradition that council-members must themselves be concerned with actual details of day to day administration.
> In consequence the larger local authorities still rely on an elaborate system of committees and sub-committees ill adapted to the mass of business . . . now requiring co-ordinated long term action.
> Paid officers are not sufficiently trusted to take action without reference to the members.
> The work is fragmented between too many separate departments, and these are seldom coherently organised or led by the Clerk.
> The result is often both inefficient and undemocratic. Members' concern with detail leaves them too little time to take the more important decisions. Officers are unable fully to exploit their powers of initiative and expert skill.[7]

Few local authorities took up this challenge, and the recommended change from obsession with overwhelming detail to purposeful impact on current problems has only gained occasional general momentum, mainly from the Bains Report[8] on management and structure for the newly created local authorities of 1973.

If local authorities, by their nature, are unable to cope with what Maud calls 'the more important decisions' they will inevitably, and rightly, continue to be superseded by other forms of central or local government. In this chapter, based on practical experience, we consider the creation of 'the more important decisions' which should constitute the council's agenda for action.

It is said that one council in Wales was so concerned to preserve and develop the use of the Welsh language in its area that it declared this to be an overriding objective, to be pursued in every activity for which it was responsible or influential. It is a clear example of a local issue being brought into the centre of the council's processes and turned into effective action. Taken seriously, such a declaration can be made to affect profoundly the way in which all services are provided, formally and informally, and also the council's internal proceedings, its recruitment and training practices, documents, sponsorships etc. It should be possible to monitor any progress achieved in pursuit of the objective and for the electorate to make a judgment for or against the council's clear stance.

In most local authorities there will be one or more local issues about which a majority of council members feel concern. Party political declarations, the regular succession of local and national elections, local pressure groups and constituency experiences will all influence the way in which councillors will approach things they want to see happen and the items which come before them. There is no shortage of the latter — the items which come unbidden on to their committee agendas. But how do councillors bring forward their own collective business agenda while also ensuring that their formal committee papers enable them to make the key decisions which will direct and control all the activities for which they are legally and politically responsible? The short answer is: by concentrating in the full council on giving clear, operationally meaningful, overall *directions*, and delegating power to carry out those *directions* to more appropriate levels of decision-making. These *directions* will be about what they want the council to achieve and about how they want the achievements to be achieved. We will use this word *directions* from now on to mean the decisions resulting from the councillors' *local political agenda*, as determined by the council, about what the organisation should achieve.

The council's *directions* — concentrating on the more important decisions

The individual councillors who comprise the council have, like a jury, to agree the arrangements under which they will operate together to discharge their responsibilities. Because local authorities are so well established, and with such a formidable accumulation of precedent, it is usual for a newly elected council to be shepherded into well-established committee sheep pens and fed a diet of consequential items flowing from the conscious or unconscious *directions* of their predecessors. They are not in control. If a council is to begin to control the vast organisation working on its behalf it must focus on the creation of a co-ordinated set of *directions* under three standard headings:

▽ *targets* for attack;
▽ *financing*;
▽ *operating values*.

Targets

The *targets* are the defined concerns of the council about which they can try to do something. They may be particular client groups in the local community, like 'the unemployed'; geographical areas, like 'Central Ward'; economic concerns like 'the development of science-based industry'; social concerns like 'crime prevention'; environmental concerns like 'better access to the countryside'. At this first political stage they are not to be confused with service targets like 'reorganisation of 16–19 education places'. The service *targets* are the means by which the service organisations will achieve the *directions* set by the council and are secondary. The *targets* for attack reflect the concerns of the councillors as elected representatives on behalf of the local community rather than as service executives, the latter being a role for which they are increasingly less appropriate as the major services lose their local basis and the need shifts to the promotion of the local dimension in nationally significant services.

Financing

The *financing* heading will show the council's stance on raising income. It will have to take into account likely income over the ensuing two to three years from government grants (difficult but not impossible to forecast), charges to clients, policy on rate levels, the potential of capital receipts and allocations, unavoidable commitments from past decisions, penalties, rate-capping etc. and now the implications of the proposed community charge and its capping. For the broad purposes of the *directions* the technical challenge, though great, is not insuperable, and the financial policies to which the council commits itself in the *directions* will give an essential basis for good operational planning.

Operating values

The *operating values* will indicate openly the council's concerns about how its activities should be conducted. The council will probably be the largest local employer and the services it provides will have some impact on every citizen. How things are done can be as important as what is achieved. Executive freedom of service committees or of operational managers will be limited, or extended, by the council's declared attitudes to contracting out, equal opportunities, redundancies, open government, decentralisation, consumerism etc.

Directions are not merely slogans expressed by resolutionary minded politicians. They are generalised, but operationally meaningful indicators for resourceful, practical action and achievement, given sufficiently in advance of executive action to enable staff, whether committees or employees, to take them into account in their operational planning. The gathering together of the council's formal decisions on these three ranges of issues in one regular, updated document should enable an elector, a councillor or an employee to know at a glance what its current policies are in practice — and take action accordingly.

The traditional alternative means having to research the bulk of detailed minutes, or trust the selective memories of other people, or find randomly distributed decisions of principle flowing from ad hoc executive decisions or from individually created departmental plans, like the 'Transport Policies and Programme' or 'Housing Improvement Plan' conceived for national grant purposes.

The council's *directions* set out under the three headings will, of course, need to be co-ordinated so that they are consistent with each other. Each of the three sets of issues is interdependent on the other two. If the council means business it will have to relate likely service expenditure to likely income and cover any likely gap by encouraging efficiency savings, making increased charges or reducing expenditure on low priority services, on a realistic timetable for achievement. Micawberish hope that 'something will turn up' to finance whatever is thought desirable is replaced by political commitment on which imaginative enterprise and achievement can be based by all those with relevant council jobs.

The raw material for defining these *directions* will be readily available in most local authorities. It is not the political or technical contents which will be new, but the processes for connecting them together and to the operational machine. Likely material for the *targets* ought to be available from the political parties' election manifestos, and from internal information like County Structure Plan monitoring reports, statistical trends plotted (a Freudian slip?) in various departmental headquarters, specially commissioned reviews of difficult subjects by committees etc., as well as White Papers and legislation.

The financial material will result from the cross-fertilisation of dominant political views on expenditure and income with professional three to four year forecasts. The significant change here will be to an open, understandable financial policy for adoption by the whole council in advance of operational planning, instead of the more usual belated annual process of last-minute deletions and cuts by the Finance Committee of whatever happens to be immediately available after a financially irresponsible parade of confrontational bidding by service departments and committees.

The challenge is to collate all this material into a format upon which the council can base credible, authoritative decisions. An actual example is given in Fig. 2. *With such a set of* directions *the council will have begun to take charge of its future.*

A sound process is needed

The staff work and organisation needed to support the council in setting *directions* is considered in the next chapter. But what process is necessary or desirable to enable the councillors to express an effective, collective will?

The three Widdicombe attributes may for this purpose be helpfully translated:

▽ political pluralism: the process must be concerned with local self-government within what the council has the constitutional power to achieve;
▽ democratic participation: the process must be concerned with engaging the support of the majority of members, despite their sectarian enthusiasms;
▽ sensitive local service delivery: the process must also be concerned with mapping clear operational objectives and constraints related to local perceptions, within which freedom to be sensitive can be exercised even more locally by those working 'at the sharp end'.

Because the *directions* have such potential significance, their approval by the council must not be just another item of routine business. Informal discussions within and between political groups and between members and officials will be a necessary part of the process. The more that ambiguity can be resolved at this stage the less it will foul implementation later. An informal seminar, available to

The Committee RECOMMENDED:

That the financial guidelines for 1984–87 encompass the intention to

(a) Maintain, and where possible, improve existing levels of service subject to radical reviews within this base level of spending and the continued vigorous pursuit of effectiveness, efficiency and innovation in delivering these services.

(b) ... etc.

(f) Update the target for further land and building sales.

1.0 SERVICE GUIDLINES

1.1 Education provision

High priority is given to standards of education. Resources will be allocated to reflect changes in pupil numbers. In order to allow the service to plan ahead in reasonable stability beyond the budget year, more detailed policies are being developed in respect of the following key areas:

(i)   teacher staffing;
(ii)   capitation;
(iii) ancillary staffing;
(iv)   further education;
(v)   under fives subject to a 'Statement'

Attention will be given to developing means of monitoring the quality of the service.

1.2 ... etc.

1.4 Economic development and unemployment

High priority is given to stimulating economic development throughout the county, capitalising on its strategic location and advanced technological capacity, but with continued emphasis on the north and east.

1.5 Road programme

Priority in the County Road Programme will be given to the completion of the primary route network.

1.6 ... etc.

2.0 AREAS FOR SCRUTINY

2.1 County property

High importance is attached to the review being undertaken by the Directorate of Land and Buildings. The purpose of the review is to achieve a better utilisation of the Authority's land and buildings. Unless a Committee can produce firm proposals for the use of property within five years, the onus will be on the responsible Committee to show why it should not be classed as surplus to requirements.

2.2 ... etc.

3.2 Effectiveness and efficiency

Committees will continue to seek ways of improving the effectiveness and efficiency of their services. High importance is attached to

(i)   the development of the Medium Term Planning process and the Performance Appraisal Scheme in improving effectiveness and

(ii) the potential of new technology for improving efficiency.

3.3 Maximising income

Committees should investigate every possibility for maximising their net income; for example, through private investment and government grants, as long as the long term implications are acceptable.

Committees in reviewing their charges should, if they are not already doing so, ascertain:

(i)   if the level of charges is appropriate;
(ii)   if the relationship between charges, levied by the Council in respect of particular client groups, is fair and consistent; and
(iii) if there are any potential new areas.

3.4 ... etc.

3.5 Use of private sector

The possibility of using the private sector should be pursued vigorously by all Committees and used when on balance benefits can be achieved.

Implementation of this guideline is left to individual Committees as circumstances permit.

'Benefits' could include savings in cost to the Authority over a reasonable period, improved levels of service, flexibility of approach, competitiveness and the stimulus to innovation.

3.6 Manpower numbers

Manpower numbers will reflect planned development. Committees will be allowed to vary their manpower beyond planned levels, provided they can prove that:

(i)   to do so will result in the better use of resources in meeting approved priorities;
(ii)   the long term implications have been taken fully into account; and
(iii) cash limits will not be exceeded.

3.7 Self-financing

Committees should undertake priority projects which will save money in the longer term. Such projects will be monitored to ensure that they do become self-financing.

Figure 2. A set of *directions*

all councillors, should be held to consider the initial collation of information and some suggested *directions*. The councillors can then expose gaps or superfluities, helpful or unhelpful presentation, and begin the informal discussions on some mutually agreed factual basis. The staccato decision-making executive committee is not the only collective mode of operation available to councillors.

Once the initial *directions* (or *guidelines* as they are more appropriately called at this early stage) have been framed by the council, the disciplines they create should then be used to evaluate and select for development the aspirations and opportunities being promoted as schemes by the council's separate departmental organisations. Given the need for emphasis on timely operational planning, the next stage is the production of a medium-term commitment plan — an annually revised set of council commitments on which practical preparations, detailed budgeting and political expectations can be safely based so long as the assumptions in the *guidelines* are not upset by a change in political control or some substantial external imperative. Should such upsets occur it is easy enough, on the basis of the existing plan, to see what can remain as council policy and what must be re-thought.

The discipline of the *guidelines* may prove inadequate or unacceptable in the face of service pressures for commitments, in which case the council can choose to amend them to square with the commitments it is prepared to approve. The integrity of the process must be preserved by continuing to match likely costs with likely income, scale of proposed activity with available time and skills, desirable activities with practically available opportunities. The *directions* and medium-term plan can then be finally approved as the practical activities which the council and its organisation is committed to achieve on a realistic time scale.

Directions and delegation — or clutter?

The council whose members and senior officers collaborate to produce a practical statement of what it currently stands for, and intends to achieve, will have begun to create an organisation which is a business-like and worthwhile instrument of local self-government. It will enable itself to fulfil the, by now familiar, Widdicombe attributes of independent local political power, exercised democratically, in the implementation of a local agenda largely through service delivery. Upon this authoritative basis the sectoral departmental oganisations are free to develop their work, subject only to control through the monitoring of their performance against the *directions* and the medium-term plan. Getting from the present state of affairs to the envisaged future is now the task to be managed, without the need for constant recourse to the council for detailed authorisation. It is a dynamic contrast to those councils whose formal agenda, policies and achievements randomly emerge from their administration of the existing organisation or from operationally unrealistic expressions of principles.

The concentration of effort required from the council and its advisers to produce this dynamic, overall framework for action, coupled with the freedom to manage its achievement sensitively to the representative nature of the council also requires the kind of purposeful, consistent scheme of delegation, of which an example is given (Fig. 3), as supplemented by any specific delegations of authority advised by the lawyers. The example is in use in a local authority which had established its *directions* and wanted to ensure that the council had the opportunity to concentrate on uncluttered primary decisions. Subordinate decisions are decen-

MEMBER FORMAL	Council	*Determine* new policy, major policy changes, major controversial matters, the constitutional framework.	
	Committees	*Determine* issues on service shape and direction subject to the council's overall policy decisions. *Recommend* major policy options to the council.	
	Sub-committees	*Determine* matters within agreed service policy where a member level decision is required. *Recommend* options on major service issues.	
MEMBER INFORMAL	Senior member Policy groups	*Plan* the approach to major issues. *Monitor* progress on the implementation of sensitive issues. *Initiate* the establishment of ad hoc informal groups of members for preliminary consideration of major issues. *Advise* chief officers on the exercise of their delegated powers.	C H I E F
	Working groups	*Investigate* specific service issues referred to them by their parent body.	O F
	Panels	*Examine* the council's activities from a client or geographical base across service boundaries — as distinct from working groups which are service based.	F I C
	Determine matters:	–Within the council's scheme of delegation to chief officers. –Concerning the implementation of agreed policies. –Of an operational nature and covered by agreed policies.	E R S

Figure 3. Scheme of delegation

tralised sensitively, but each within the framework set by more senior levels. The overriding local political issues are concentrated for debate as initiatives by the council, rather than as belated consequences of unwelcome interference in day-to-day executive management.

The alternative is a clutter:

▽   of ad hoc decisions of varying importance and clarity, randomly distributed through volumes of minutes of the proceedings of previous committees and councils;
▽   of current operational dilemmas arising from lack of clarity in the direction of the existing service organisations;
▽   of incompatible management information and working practices developed in the separate departments;
▽   of 'seat of the pants' management in executive committees;
▽   of issues being unselectively processed upwards to the highest levels of decision-making on the vague justification that this is 'democratic'.

It is a recipe for confusion.

Detail and democracy

Because the council is a corporate body with total responsibility for all its multifarious activities carried out by hundreds, thousands, tens of thousands of employees, the 'democratic' argument is often used to justify it making as many decisions as possible — though it is often no more than a knee-jerk defence of the *status quo*. The snag is that it is just not practicable, if the function of the council in determining local political issues and controlling the whole of its organisation's activities (not just the currently high profile ones) is to avoid being swamped.

There is a cost to the extra element of democracy which is present in a local authority, as distinct from other forms of local government. In considering the appropriateness of democratic control, as a desirable means of local government, or in using the democratic processes of a local authority, that cost should be justified by the greater value which democracy has added. Economy and efficiency gained in an appointed Quango by more easily focused *directions* than is usually possible in a representative body will be of little value if the product fails to meet what local people really need. Local democracy has a potentially valuable contribution to make to local government; it must not squander its opportunities. We all know of councils with monthly meetings that consist of little more than a constant parade of random executive decisions to be endorsed where the relevant committee has lacked the delegated power to take its own initiative. When challenged, the people concerned excuse themselves on the vague basis that 'the council must be seen to be democratic' or 'there's no chance of finding common ground — it's a case of political point-scoring and always will be'. This lack of courage (and sometimes of ability) to address the needs for which the council has a responbility is an abuse of democracy which adds to waste and irrelevance.

In the days

▽   when councils were responsible for providing a smaller range of less complex services to smaller populations;
▽   when aldermen and less volatile local election voting patterns produced a longer collective memory in the council; and especially

▽   when ever-increasing government grants made it easier to match political aspirations with resources;

it is possible that a council's implicit, overall intentions were better understood by
the public, by the councillors when in a committee, and by the employees. The
formal processes then in standard use for focusing on a co-ordinated approach to
the future were the reporting of all committee business as recommendations for
final decision by the council, and the annual authorisation by the council of expenditure in the budget, both processes being subject to the informal co-ordination of
any local party machinery or the general sense of the more senior members.

It is important to see the traditional decision-making processes in this context
if we are to understand why they are now defective. Delegation of service-based
decision-making to 'service committees' without constant recourse to the council
as a whole, made necessary by the increased volume and complexity of business,
leads to an unhealthy domination of the council's work and processes by ad hoc
narrow service management issues. The more the separated service interests
gather individual momentum, the more difficult it becomes for the council to act
other than with the grain of the services, despite the councillors' democratic origins and despite the enormous weight of resources and range of service impact on
local problems nominally available to them collectively. Sub-committees of a policy committee, for example, may be set up for performance review, personnel
etc., or special working parties may be instituted to pursue specific topics, but any
conclusions they reach will usually be kept at bay by the service committees as
untimely and unsympathetic 'central interference' which, given the traditional
processes of executive decision-making, they frequently are! Only the financial
control is capable of surviving in strength because it stems from the corporate
budget which the council as a whole has to make.

But a tighter financial situation, arising largely from the rapid and erratic
annual reduction in government grant and rate capping, makes the annual budget
process unsuitably late to change most existing financial commitments for the
ensuing financial year. The combination of the two — service-based decision-
making and an untimely financial planning process — inevitably leads to short-
term financial expedients, while the likelihood of redundant or low-priority
expenditure is in practice unacknowledged and its considerable potential is
unexplored.

Since the council in its own meetings obviously cannot make all the decisions
that must be made in its name with a sense of continuity and purpose, then the
challenge is to create a council-backed programme of activity which the council
can control, leaving to subordinate committees and employees the freedom to
make consequential decisions within that control. This is democratic!

Questions

▲   *1. Taking the issue in the local community which you identified when dealing with
Question 1 of Chapter 1 on page 14, what are the council's current* directions *about
it to those who operate on the council's behalf?*

▲   *2. Are these* directions *clear enough to control what is done to achieve them? Are
they clear enough to enable performance measures to be used to demonstrate the extent of achievement?*

▲ *3. If the council's* directions *were better articulated, co-ordinated and communicated, what scope would there then be for clarifying and developing structures, jobs and processes to improve the pace and quality of achievements?*

▲ *4. Try tackling Checklist Two on page 121.*

5   The headquarters organisation

Local authority politics should be about linking political ideals with local data to produce practical results within the scope of the council's powers. There is no lack of available local data, but the information needs organising to be digestible. The chief executive must carry this responsibility, as head of the corporate 'staff'. The distinction between 'staff' and 'line' responsibilities, often held in the same job, must be clear if corporate information, and control of and support to those in the 'line' are to be managed effectively. Unfortunately, traditional organisation prevents effective management of 'staff' work. The same principles apply to the jobs to which the council appoints councillors! They too, should have their 'staff' and 'line' responsibilities clearly defined.

Politics must be linked to facts to produce practical results

Modern local authorities trace their organisational origins back directly to the local initiatives of the newly industrialised urban communities which became recognised in the Municipal Corporations Act, 1835. Their purposes were made clear in the powers they were granted to deal with nationally acknowledged local problems — problems identified by local leaders through a mixture of indignation, common sense and idealism. Yet we should not under-estimate the complexity of their world, nor the degree of research and practical knowledge which was necessary to translate that indignation, common sense and idealism into successful solutions which we now treat as obvious. In *A Century of Municipal Progress*, Professor Smith refers to the plague which in 1832 decimated the inhabitants of the over-crowded and insanitary slums of Manchester. A young local physician, Dr Kay, wrote a pamphlet describing the appalling local conditions and, in 1833, helped to found the Manchester Statistical Society as 'an expression of the growing view that social and political theories must be tested by facts, and that scientific and large-scale inquiry must guide the formulation of remedies'. Its five founders were two bankers, two cotton manufacturers, and Dr Kay himself, and four of them were under thirty years of age. The first members included many who were destined to play a prominent part in local and national government. One of the earliest inquiries of the Society was into the state of education in Manchester. They knew the problem; they knew the solutions available; and they knew the results they wanted.

The desirability of a modern council setting out clearly its purposes and commitments in a concise statement of *directions* and a medium-term plan is easy to appreciate; but how is it to be achieved in an operationally meaningful form, in practice? A collection of slogans, however expressive of feelings within a political group, will, at best, do little more than indicate a general approach and some 'no-go areas'. 'Value for money', for example, or 'working for the community' are fine sentiments but convey little to the public, the council's committees or the council's employees about hard-edged action. Indeed, if they are left as slogans without realistic plans for achievement they risk misinterpretation or incomprehension from all those people who are involved as electors, clients, councillors or employees.

Nor should the practical provision of the council's services to the public continue in a political vacuum, whether that provision is called 'administration' or the currently more fashionable 'management', as if these were ends in themselves. In the absence of the council's current *directions* and commitments, whose are the purposes, values and interests being implicitly pursued in all the many decisions that are being made daily on the council's behalf, with its authority but without its knowledge?

Our Victorian forebears carved out initiatives and legal powers, creating their own freedoms to act with, as yet, small resources in their employment. Now, those resources are enormous but the energies of local authorities have become more concerned about maintaining them than about using them to make relevant impacts on current problems.

So this chapter is about harnessing the enormous resources of legal powers, finance, property and skills available to the council, and linking them to that mixture of indignation, common sense and idealism which the electorate has endorsed. The end product is what we described earlier as the council's *local political agenda* whose determination was discussed in the last chapter.

The organisation knows a lot about the local community

Information of many kinds is constantly being gathered and sifted by the council's employees for a variety of purposes. The availability of information, even of relevant information, is not usually a problem; it is there in quantity. General community-based data will be available in the Planning Department or Corporate Planning Unit; individual service-based data will be available in each service department; financial data in the Finance Department . . . and so on. The large size and fast changing nature of the communities governed by local councils make it worthwhile to supplement the opinions of the elected members by drawing on this mass of information about what is going on in the community. The large size, individual historic development, pre-determined scope and confused central/local government financial and operational controls of the major services make it impossible for members to comprehend unaided the possibilities realistically available to them by way of direct control or of influence on local problems.

In addition to the ideas which the councillors themselves bring to the process of *direction* setting and medium-term planning there are, therefore, two particular strands of information which the senior advisers of the council should produce:

▽   significant trends observable in the local community;
▽   operational limits on political options.

To these must ultimately be added a third strand, which is dealt with in Chapter 9:

▽   the results currently being achieved by the council.

The task of gathering relevant information together, presenting it in a digestible form which is free of service jargon, and mutually compatible so as to enable comparison and connections to be validly made, requires considerable organisation. And because the information will often come from a source with a vested interest in the outcome of the process for establishing *directions* and medium-term planning, it is necessary to build in adequate validation if it is to be used with confidence among inevitable controversy.

It is not only the confidence of the councillors involved in the political arguments that matters. Because the major purpose of the process is concerned with practical achievements, the information must also carry the confidence of the people whose work the council is seeking to direct and control. So the task of gathering, validating, editing and presenting the information must be clearly defined in advance with the methods regularly and openly reviewed and widely disseminated throughout the council's management structure.

But the raw information is indigestible

How, then, do we create an authoritative process for supplying the councillors with the corporate information they need to determine the council's *directions* and medium-term plan from such a jumble of different sources? Effective preparation for action by the complex organisation of a local authority is about integration:

▽   of the political insights which fuel the concerns of the people who offer themselves for election;

▽   of the vast amounts of otherwise underused knowledge gained by employees in the course of their work;

▽   of the corporate management information separately held in different departments and sections;

▽   of the changing perceptions of the councillors, gathered from their own links with the electorate and political organisation outside the council, as well as from their own views of the council's effectiveness.

The secret of successful integration is primarily to do with the processing of the information across the council and its management structure, rather than with the restructuring of committees and departments — though the latter may be shown by the process to be necessary. Certainly there must be a clear responsibility pinned down somewhere for the effectiveness of the information supply — it will not just happen by itself.

Historically, the departmental structure of local authorities has developed under the jealous and defensive eye of the particular profession dominating each department . . . and if there wasn't a relevant profession, one was soon created.

This tradition of separate departmental development has led to a situation in which co-ordination and the assertion of the council's essential unity has to be forced across rather than with the grain of the organisation. Until the Bains Report in 1972, the received wisdom in local authorities was that the town or county clerk was, in relation to the other chief officers, 'first among equals' — a statement of such organisational nonsense that it was usually expressed by the clerks in Latin and interpreted in practice according to force of personality and political support from leading members.

The chief executive as 'chief of staff'

Based on a few brave experiments, the Bains Report (following the Maud Report on Management in 1967) recommended the establishment in the reorganised local authorities of a clearly designated head of the council's paid service — the chief executive. Almost all councils now have such a post, and the task of ensuring good quality, co-ordinated, corporate advice to the council in the preparation of their *directions* and medium-term plan is clearly one for that post holder. The process of preparation is not merely mechanical in nature, but involves taking account of the politics, personalities and history of the council as well as the raw data. The successful organisation of the supply of information, against the weighty but narrow and separate loyalties of departments and their related committees, requires a radical rethink about the function the chief executive is there to fulfil, and about the resources needed for the task. There are too many casualties in this job for complacency about defining its agreed purpose.

The issue is relevant not just to this one responsibility of corporate information supply but to all aspects of work which involve the assertion of the council's primacy over the organisation which is there to serve it. It is conveniently dealt with here, however, in relation to the task of helping the council to create its corporate will and commitment in operationally meaningful terms. This corporate will is the foundation for the chief executive's role as the council's 'chief of staff'.

A common approach gives to the chief executive a 'corporate planning unit' to add to the miscellaneous functions inherited from the old clerk of the council, and any other functions generated independently of the other departments which may have been added because of the importance at one time attached to them, such as 'economic development' or 'value for money reviews'. The danger with this approach is that either the unit tries to comprehend the job on its own, thus losing the creative involvement of relevant knowledge and skills in other departments, or it duplicates the planning work carried out in other departments by constituting an additional, and largely unnecessary, layer of co-ordination. Sometimes it manages to do both! The provision of 'co-ordinative staff' to deal with co-ordinative staff should always be rigorously questioned. So what we are seeking is a tauter line management of the co-ordination, control and support functions carried out by such specialist skills as, for example, architecture, personnel, finance, corporate planning and the advisory functions of the service departments. This can only be achieved by retuning the existing lines of professional networks, which only co-operate through the consent of their separate professional hierarchies, to a more harmonious support of the chief executive in ensuring the supply of sound, relevant, official, corporate information to the council. In return, the departments involved are assured of a voice in the process which will determine the *directions* and specific commitments approved by the council. Once loyalty to and accountability for the corporate process transcends narrow departmental loyalties and personal rivalries, the narrow departmental base of those with the skills required to devise, maintain, improve and supply the processes will be relevant only to professional standards.

The distinction between 'staff' and 'line'

What we are concerned with here is the chief executive in his capacity as chief of the council's 'staff' — using the word 'staff' in the sense of the necessary intermediaries between those in command, the council, and those who carry out the orders. Their function is to help the council direct and control the 'line' managers of teachers, social workers and all other employees who produce the council's direct services for its public, and the external contractors whose services are brought in. This 'staff' function of interpretation, monitoring and advice requires its own 'line' management, just as the 'line' managers of the direct service providers will almost invariably have a 'staff' function too. The city solicitor is a 'staff' officer to the council in giving legal advice; he is a 'line' manager in organising the production of the advice. The county surveyor is a 'line' manager for the purpose of building roads, but has (or should have!) a 'staff' function in advising the council on all their transport-related decisions, and not just the ones related to his own line management. It is important to recognise the different elements in the same person's job when considering who should be involved in a 'staff' process, if maximum synergy from several people is to be achieved.

Since the Bains Report laid the foundations for much good current organisation in local authorities, there has developed an increasingly widespread recognition that certain departments are different in their general nature from others. Some are overwhelmingly 'line' and others are overwhelmingly 'staff' as viewed by the council. But such a distinction at departmental level will be fairly crude; the Engineer's Department may advise in a 'staff' way on council vehicles generally and the Secretary's Department may 'line' manage a land charges service to the public. Even more importantly, the policy advice potentially available in every service department is a vital 'staff' function which ought to be engaged in an integrated way if the council is to be supported effectively.

In practice, however, departments are dubbed either 'staff' or 'line', with the 'staff' departments increasingly referred to as the 'central' departments, in an attempt to recognise their all-pervasive involvement in the council's affairs. Such departments include architect's, central purchasing, chief executive's, corporate planning, land agent's, personnel, secretary's, treasurer's. Yet the director of housing or of social services ought to be as much a part of any 'centre' as the treasurer or architect — more so, in fact, because the public services they provide are at the centre of the council's concerns.

The fact that this is so often not the case reflects not only the centralist elitism which has kept the most influential policy advisory roles as the almost exclusive preserve first of the lawyers, and now also of the accountants, but also the reluctance of many of the service managers to engage themselves, their people, their information or their commitment to the 'central' processes, such as financial planning which, as they see it, are other people's problems which threaten their freedom to manage. The result is an artificial and unhelpful separation of the 'staff' function not just into separate departments, but into an artificially exclusive 'centre' separated from the activities which express the council's will in practical services. Unless this separation is overcome, the recruitment of future chief executives will continue to be confined to a very limited range of experiences and corporate synergy will be much less than it ought to be.

The council's control of the 'line' through 'staff'

The problem of creating a tautly managed 'staff' is not principally one of internal pecking orders, however, or of semantics. We are trying to create a central, supportive process for helping the councillors collectively to produce a co-ordinated statement of *directions* and commitments to govern the operations of the organisation and on which corporate controls can be based. The service departments are as essential to the effectiveness of such a process as these 'central' departments. So why make a distinction between them?

The reason is pragmatic, based on a need to start the co-ordination of the potential 'staff' function at a stage which reflects present reality. Once the existing separations have been effectively overcome at the most senior level, the rest will follow the lead.

Given the responsibility of the chief executive for producing co-ordinated official advice to the council, and for ensuring that its corporate decisions are carried out (yet recognising the distinctive traditions and features of the separate major services) the pragmatic matrix in Fig. 4 can usefully be employed to help begin to sort out the different inter-relationships that are needed at the most senior levels of 'staff' work.

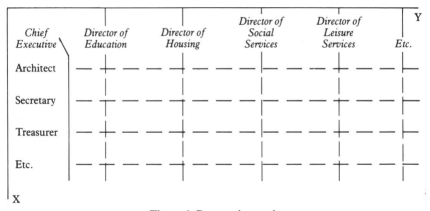

Figure 4. Pragmatic matrix

This arrangement highlights the chief executive's role in establishing tight overall line management of the corporately significant 'staff' departments along the X axis, and of these departments' involvement in corporate issues with their counterpart service managers on the Y axis. The linking of each X axis staff function with each Y axis service on the matrix raises questions about the effectiveness of, say, the links between the property and the social services departments in pursuit of a co-ordinated 'staff' function from which action can flow efficiently and effectively in managing properly the property resources allocated by the council to social services.

The only justification for such a crude matrix is its use as a starting point for organising support to the collective deliberations and decisions of the members, so that the council can assert its corporate will over its otherwise separate activities. The pre-eminent responsibilities of the chief executive, and the critically important links between him and those who lead the council politically, arise not from a personal power base but from the council's need for the co-ordination of official advice and for the implementation of its *directions* on the basis of its commitments. If the council is little more than a court of highest appeal on issues arising ad hoc from the operations of the several departments, then it may be questioned whether anything very different from the administrative co-ordination of the old-style clerk is necessary.

The matrix is a starting point only, and the allocation of departments, or significant sections of departments, to one axis or the other may give rise to questions about the large number of separate 'staff' groups there are in the authority. In Chapter 9 of the Bains Report ('The new authorities — Functions and possible management'), no distinction was made between X and Y type chief officers, but the obvious candidates for the X axis in any of the Report's suggested structures are never less than half the number of obvious candidates for the Y axis, and usually almost the same number. This is absurd — yet it is common practice, and the root cause of inadequate 'staff' co-ordination.

Running the X axis functions across the individual Y axis service departments may also give rise to questions about the effectiveness of the functional distribution. In how many service departments is there second-rate financial expertise, which is then carefully checked in an over-qualified finance department, because isolationism in the service department, or the service department's fear of 'empire building' by the finance department, prevents sensible out-posting from the finance to the service department? In how many departments is there sound personnel advice available on a basis which maintains corporate consistency, yet with only exceptional need to check back with 'central personnel'? To what extent is less costly and better advice available from external sources — a consultancy or another local authority's experts — rather than assuming 'in-house' is the only way to provide support?

The precise form of the X axis organisation will depend on local personalities and circumstances, but clearly there is advantage in reducing formal groupings to the minimum consistent with good line management. However, no formal organisation will, of itself, achieve co-ordination of all these activities. The political themes which dominate the work required will vary from time to time. The need for tighter financial management, followed by the search for value for money, then decentralisation of decision-making, then more positive motivation through personnel policies is not an unusual progression. Moreover, the annual corporate processes for *direction* setting, medium-term planning and the budget will create their own changing demands for co-operative work across internal professional and organisational boundaries. The objective of co-ordinating the X axis and its inter-relationships with the Y axis is to enable the chief executive to utilise these corporately significant skills with the minimum of organisational obstruction and professional time. For the purposes of corporate advice and control, the heads of all departments are all the deputies of the chief executive, in the sense of accepting responsibility for the success of the whole co-ordinative processes at officer level.

The co-ordinative processes should not become a new additional burden of work (except during their original creation), but a more purposeful and open way of responding operationally to the council's determination to create its own *local political agenda*, by better organisation of what already exists in fragmented, duplicated and rival ways.

Presentation to and digestion of corporate information by councillors

Once the information has been prepared, it must be presented to the members for consideration and decision. Again the official process must be carefully designed to meet the actual needs and constraints of the people involved if they are to lead to a result on which subsequent control and initiatives can be soundly based. The oral presentation of the written papers collated, edited and validated from a wide range of official sources will be a splendid test of the corporateness achieved by the chief executive in the preparatory process. Will the chief executive, or his representative, be trusted to give necessarily selective emphasis to some parts of the material? Will each department insist on being represented at all stages, so that employees outnumber the councillors, and technical detail or minor operational problems obscure the major political issues? Will one of the X axis staff officers, such as the treasurer, want to present an 'independent' view? Will the councillors in a minority grouping, who find the information uncongenial, be able to challenge its objectivity? Will the majority group impatiently dismiss operational factors that would get in their way?

Or will a process of informal, responsible negotiation and bargaining take place before decisions are finally made, albeit one which may stretch both the patience of members wanting achievements quickly and inexpensively, and the courage of officers reluctant to promise what they are doubtful about achieving? Unless the integrity and fairness of the preparatory process are widely accepted, there is little hope of creating synergy in the council's organisation — and unless the process has helped to create an overall impact on the local community's problems greater than the sum of the council's separate services, it will not have been worthwhile. Where the process encourages the employees to respect the role of councillors in choosing what they, collectively, want to happen, and the councillors to respect the practical constraints on those who are employed to make things happen, and where genuine political controversy is identified and resolved separately from the management of implementation, there should be achieved an effective harnessing of the council's organisation to its political will and from which dynamic local government can result. The secret agenda of sectional enthusiasts, wriggled through an overcluttered succession of ad hoc items for decision, no longer have a place.

In commenting on the co-ordination of the council's 'staff', we have concentrated only on the staff work and responsibilities of the employees. But the council also appoints its own members to jobs such as committee member, and these have collective 'staff' and 'line' elements too. The freedom of being a councillor in one way is limited only by legislation and the standing orders of the council, but the job of a committee member is almost wholly determinable by the council. No councillor has a right or an obligation to be on a committee and, subject to a few legal requirements, the functions of any committee will be as the council has determined them. All the need for co-ordination of the employee 'staff' applies with similar force to this subordinate member organisation. We will examine the implications of the 'line management' role of committees in the next chapter but their 'staff' role is pursued here.

The committee equivalent of the X axis in Fig. 4 will usually be the 'policy' committee. The policy committee is therefore in a broadly similar position vis-à-vis the service committees as is the chief executive to the service chief officers. The parallel is even clearer if the policy sub-committees relate, in name and function, to the chief officers shown on the X axis.

Just as the Chief Executive's power within the employee structures should rest on the policy *directions* and commitments of the council, so should the power of the policy committee. If it does not it is likely to become a rag bag of odds and ends which cannot be fitted into another committee's work, and a source of irritation by guessing the work of the other committees, unaided by authoritative council guidance. 'Is a policy committee really necessary?' is a legitimate question.

What would be missing if it did not exist?

Once its 'staff' role is positively appreciated, its main purposes can be seen to include:

▽ the promotion of overall organisational health to enable the council's will to be effective;

▽ the supervision of the major policy planning and resource allocation processes;

▽ the formalisation of big issues for determination by the council;

▽ the monitoring of performance against the council's programmes.

Achieving practical success in these purposes will depend heavily on the extent to which the policy committee or some informal equivalent is able to assist the council in co-ordinating the separate strands of political staff work, and the political with the employee staff work.

The 'staff' contribution of the other committees will depend upon the processes which the council creates to enable them to have an effective part to play in the *directional* issues. This raises one particular criterion for shaping the committee structure: the need for evenness in 'political clout', to ensure equity in the overall treatment of competing claims for resources. In a local authority where each professional service has 'its own committee', the danger will be that the more significant committees will attract the more experienced and able councillors as well as constituting a larger voting bloc of service enthusiasts in the full council meeting. To ensure integrity of approach in weighing the community's need of a public library, a school or a fire station etc., consistently with the council's *directions*, the distribution of councillors to service committees needs to avoid dominance by the education lobby (purely by way of example!) just because it is bigger than the fire committee. It is the council's overall political role which should dominate the shape of its committee structure, not its questionable involvement in executive management. If the council is to be more than the sum of its parts, its structure should not inhibit the transfer of resources from one service to another, nor obscure the broad vision for the future which the council as a whole is there to develop on behalf of the local community.

Questions

▲ 1. *'The availability of information . . . is not usually a problem' (page 44). Take the issues you have already identified as being important to the council in Question 1 of Chapter 1 on page 14, and now identify all sources of relevant information readily available within the organisation. How could it most helpfully be presented to the council?*

▲ 2. *Consider the matrix set out on page 48. Allocate the departments in your organisation to the X or Y matrix. Take the department you know best. How could its contribution to corporate 'staff' work be improved?*

▲ 3. *What new or improved processes are needed to enable the council to digest co-ordinated management information when making decisions?*

6   Organising for results

A committee should primarily be concerned with workable strategies for achieving the results the council has indicated in its *directions*. This includes choosing the most suitable agencies, not just passively accepting the existing arrangements for service delivery. The formal committee structure is partly fixed by law but should be consciously shaped to cope with the council's current concerns. So should the committees' business, to reflect the whole of the work delegated by the council, including the whole of the in-house service work. This will need good 'staff' support to provide the appropriate management information; and conscious distancing of committees from detailed operational decisions. The councillors must control their own opportunities if they wish to promote real local democracy.

The committee role in line management is primarily about a practical strategy

In Chapter 4 we considered the council's responsibility to determine a *local political agenda* to govern the local authority's work. We encouraged the council to be pro-active, initiating activity to meet the local community's current needs as the council saw them, instead of being overwhelmed by random reactions to the needs of its inherited 'services'.

These 'services', such as education, housing, refuse collection, libraries etc., are the creation of previous councils for meeting local needs, and they remain important contributors to contemporary life, if they can be controlled to fix their priority and to maintain their quality and relevance. In practice, their public importance and sheer size tend to dominate the councillors' decision-making processes, crowding out opportunities for thinking more widely than the immediate needs of the services, or for thinking ahead — or even for controlling effectively the work which the services do. The question has to be asked: is a committee of lay councillors able to fulfil a proper role in line management beyond the most senior level of general direction and the monitoring of overall performance? The question whether local democracy fulfils a valuable role at all in relation to the provision of nationally standard services takes us back to the basic purposes of a local authority and the need to demonstrate their value.

The kind of education which will best meet the local community's current and future needs, or the views of local employers and recent school leavers on the appropriateness of local education, are much more appropriate leads into local democratic deliberation than choosing a school caretaker, deciding some unusual point about school transport, or fixing the grade of clerical staff. Concerns about the local economy, about juvenile crime, about promotion of the arts, and any other concerns about the local community, can be woven into a strategy for action, resulting from and influencing the council's overall *directions*. The council and its committees can then directly make rational and systematic use of the skills, powers and resources made available to them and can direct influence to where central government or other agencies are making the controlling decisions. Just as the council's *direction*-setting should not be dominated by the requirements of service management, neither should the strategy making by the council's committees for the achievement of those *directions*. The need for service management to obtain executive authorisations traditionally provides convenient pegs on which to hang ad hoc attempts at direction and strategy by councillors, but the result is likely to be confused, belated and only incidental to the effective control of the services' established momentum. As the policies and practices of traditional local authority services move increasingly towards a national basis with local sensitivity provided by school governors, urban development corporations and other forms of local government, the democratic local processes must find new ways of being effective.

Where the council does assert its overall will by way of *directions* and commitments, the committees can be used to earth the discussions at council level because of their members' more practical experience in implementing the council's will. This 'staff' function of support to the council flows from its 'line management' function of devising and pursuing strategies to achieve acceptable results related to the council's *directions*.

The committee level of decision-making may usefully be considered as an opportunity for collective thought before and after the broad *direction* setting of the council, based on more detailed exposure to implementation and service delivery. It is a place where councillors can, if they wish, shape the strategies for achieving the council's wishes within the resources made available by the council, on the basis of a more detailed examination of the management information used by it in arriving at its *directions*. It is also the place for key democratic control of the service organisations. It should not be a place where supporters of a particular enthusiasm are enabled to badger and bargain for some specific action irrespective of relevance to corporate priorities, available resources, professional advice or better strategic options. The 'bottom up' organisational pressures must be dealt with as a consequence of the committee's interpretation of the council's 'top down' *directions*. It should not be a bazaar!

Too often a committee is pressed into approving, say, a new village bypass, when a more careful look at the primary road network would have led to a co-ordinated, consistent strategy over several years for major capital road works which — because they are co-ordinated — may well shift the weight of traffic away from that village, and several others too. In the absence of such a co-ordinated strategy, it is difficult to see how a committee can deal with ad hoc pressures for improvements, other than succumb to them!

Instead of a proposed school closure being debated in isolation from any overall strategy for providing better education within available resources, the understandable concerns of local pressure groups can be weighed against the loss of the more general benefits of a consciously approved strategy for redirecting the resources wastefully consumed by the underused buildings. The democratic process should not be just about the exceptional.

The sources of the committee's management information will be the same as those used by the council in setting its *directions*, because the committee will have contributed to the council's current *directions* and commitments, and will be preparing for the next annual round of reconsideration and amendment. The committee will itself require 'staff' support, tautly managed to provide integration and consistency with the broader *direction*-setting level at this more strategic operational level. From this information the committee can develop its own relevant *targets*, financial commitments and working methods within those set by the council. The committee can initiate and prioritise activity, instead of simply responding to the ad hoc pressures surrounding 'its' departments.

The spur to encourage a committee to face these difficult issues, instead of coming to the council each budget time with a begging bowl and a string of pathetic requirements, is the realistic limit on medium-term resources which the council will have fixed by bringing together its financial and operational planning. Such a discipline is even more effective if the council permits operational savings to be used by the committee responsible for achieving them, instead of counter-productively creaming them off into general funds.

Implementing the strategies

In making the first moves to implement the chosen strategies, the key questions are:

▽   what agencies shall we use?
▽   how shall we monitor their performance?

For the council and its committees are not confined to act solely through the parts of the council's organisation which they directly control. Given an effective corporate 'staff' approach linked to effective corporate political processes, there is the potential of contributions from several departments and from other agencies — other local authorities, other public bodies, private ventures with relevant expertise, voluntary agencies, even the ogre of central government. The committee will be able to serve the council's purposes by co-ordinating the use of these other agencies to supplement or replace the council's own permanent organisation wherever there is advantage. Understanding the arcane mysteries of spoilt votes, for example, need not be kept fresh at County Hall for an election once every four years when the skill is replicated in each district authority for more frequent use. The highway agency, claimed as of right by many a district council, may be an expensive way of providing an inefficient service to the public, given the economy of scale and continuity which ought to be available to the county surveyor. The balance of full-time/retained firemen makes a major contribution to cost-effectiveness where local authorities are prepared to pursue the options thoroughly and purposefully. The regional water authority's plans will crucially affect the practicality of the County Structure Plan. Joint planning and joint finance with the health service are a universal feature of social services strategy. Public librarians are increasingly involved in co-ordinating the resources of university and other local specialist libraries to complement the local authority library service to the public. Sponsorship of the local Marriage Guidance Council, Citizens' Advice Bureau and other volunteer agencies is commonplace. Proposed legislation consciously promotes alternative means of providing housing and schools. Most of these methods are available without even considering any advantages in 'contracting out' to the private sector, but while use of other agencies to achieve council objectives is no novelty to local authorities, it often looks like an afterthought. Only when the choice of agency has been determined does a third key question arise:

▽   how can we ensure the sensitive management of our 'in-house service(s)'? —
     a question discussed in the next chapter.

As a theoretical exercise, it is worth taking the council's *directions* and work-ing out how to implement them without making use of its own service delivery organisation. After all, comparatively little of the central government's pro-gramme of local services was, until recently, directly provided by the govern-ment. Improving the quality of local education becomes the challenge, rather than 'running' the LEA schools; exposing the causes of 'traffic congestion' has pre-cedence over the priority of randomly advocated roadworks. Practical concern about the quality of employees replaces eccentric plunges into grading appeals or cuts in the all too readily available training fund. Of course, the advantages of the council's statutory powers to do things directly will soon become apparent in such an exercise, but the direct provision is put in a purposeful context.

Organising the committee structure

The device of creating a standing committee to specialise in some particular part of the council's responsibilities goes back many years — so much so that educa-tion, police and social services committees have, by law, to be appointed and, at any rate until very recently, it has been standard practice for each service to have a related and separate committee.

The now common practice of the council delegating wide powers to such committees is more recent, the theory having been that the council's formal ap-proval of its committees' recommendations provided the necessary co-ordination and gave all councillors an opportunity to be involved in what was being decided. In practice, the adoption of most recommendations was a formality and the service committee/service department link became the strongest feature of local authority structures, processes and decision-making. Our proposals for council-created direction and commitments are intended to provide a background of positive, corporate co-ordination with which to contain and shape this executive service domination of the local political process. But they will only do so if the committee structure and functions observe the discipline which the *directions* and medium-term plan create.

The choice of a committee structure should reflect the council's current con-cerns:

▽   for its collective decision-making to be carried out formally and publicly;
▽   for adequate exploration of the options available to fulfil its overall *directions*;
▽   for the effective direction of its accumulated, inherited services; and
▽   for ensuring the sensitive management of these services.

One possibility is to establish a committee structure with responsibilities grouped to reflect the priorities of the council's *directions*, irrespective of relation-ship to the service departments. The main political drives behind the council's *di-rections* will certainly show the local issues which concern it, but merely creating a formal committee structure based on topics like, for example, 'social integration', 'rural transport needs' or 'anti-poverty' is likely to lead to confusion of responsibil-ity for political *directions* of services — and to lack of operational response from the services themselves unless the 'staff' function of preparation and co-ordination de-scribed in the last chapter is well developed.

The objection to a service-based structure, on the other hand, has the disad-vantage that it encourages further separation of the already too separate profes-sional thinking and action of each service. Provided that the strong arrangements for an effective 'staff' function are made, this objection is substantially overcome. A service-based committee structure can work satisfactorily if the service core of work is accepted as a consequential stage in the achievement of the council's *directions*, each committee working out an operational strategy in which service organisation is used, along with other selected agencies, as a means to the council's ends. The service committee is not intended to be the democratic icing on a professionally predetermined piece of cake!

In practice, the legal requirements to establish education, police and social service committees must have a major impact on the structure of many local authorities. Moreover, the sheer weight of the services as major, established organisations for dealing with defined local needs, the frequent lack of clear line management in each service capable of interacting with good council 'staff' work (see Chapters 5 and 7) and the force of traditional public perceptions, will all tend to favour a service-based committee structure.

Not that we are advocating a separate committee for each separate service. In the last chapter we referred to the desirability of evenness in the 'political clout' of the various service committees, to ensure equity in the treatment of the competing claims for resources. Rather than have a separate but not very influential libraries committee, why not decide whether the library service is there substantially to fulfil the council's educational concerns — in which case, link its work to the control of the education committee. If, however, its function is seen differently, e.g. as a leisure pursuit, then link it with a committee which controls the council's leisure services — which may again be education, or may be parks, entertainments etc. Between the extremes of a committee for each service and a committee for each local priority issue is a pragmatic matching of issues to services, with special provision for good 'staff' work when an issue spans more than one service.

A particularly adventurous solution would be for the democratic control of the provision of services to be undertaken by a very small number of councillors in each service committee, with the remaining councillors active in issue-based committees linked to the council's current concerns. Such an arrangement would increase the influence of councillors on overall *directions* (assuming that the council has a process for setting *directions*) and remove a great deal of time-consuming managerial business from the inappropriate processes of large executive committees. The small service committees would provide political backing to, and accountability for, the work of service provision within the framework of the council's *directions* and of budgetary and other information systems designed to expose performance against pre-set objectives. Such an arrangement would also highlight the need for the kind of systematic scheme of delegation to which we referred on page 39.

Agenda preparation

The overall processes of the council will always dictate consequences for its committees' business. The traditional budget process, for example, automatically involves committees in a bidding process. A *direction*-setting process should also involve the committees in their 'staff' role, and as part of its 'staff' function a committee can try to persuade the council to modify these overall processes if it considers they lead to an inadequate formal agenda. The rest of the committees' agendas will, in the absence of any further requirements of the council, be a mixture of items raised by the chief officers, by a political group or by individual councillors; or they will be the reports of sub-committees. Devices for helping a committee to control the construction of its agendas are:

▽   for the committee itself to take time at its first meeting of the local authority's year to plan how it will spend its time, having regard to the council's overall processes, outstanding political issues, and its own responsibilities for achieving the council's *directions*, and for ensuring the sensitive management of its directly accountable 'in-house' services. It can then marshal its own programme and that of its sub-committees in accordance with the council's scheme of delegation;

▽   for the committee's secretariat to keep agenda plans so that congestion is spotted in advance, so that important items get priority, and items of doubtful value are referred to other processes.

In practice, the allocation of business to different levels of decision-making is often not as cut-and-dried as theory might suggest. However clear the council's scheme of delegation, however purposeful the committee has been in planning the major items for its agendas and however skilful its secretariat may be, there will frequently be ambiguous situations requiring an authoritative decision about what to place, or what not to place, on an agenda. The extent of public pressure, or the political influence of an individual, can often turn an operational detail rightly or wrongly into a major controversy. Yet asking the committee to decide whether it wishes to discuss the item will defeat the very purpose of trying to avoid clutter.

What if a member or a chief officer wishes to challenge the continued wisdom of an established *direction*? What if a political group wishes to raise a new issue outside the pre-determined timetable? What if members are concerned about the adequacy of key employees? What if the officers advising the committee seem unable to subordinate their departmental and professional loyalties to their 'staff' responsibilities to the council? What if a councillor insists on taking a local complaint to the committee before exhausting other processes?

Questions of this kind are traditionally dealt with by the chairman and by discussion with other key councillors, but just because the situation is ambiguous the chairman may be strongly tempted to take a line of least resistance. There is merit in formally organising a gateway between the committee and the politically significant activities of its related department(s) by deliberately and openly creating a small representative group of key councillors and key 'staff' at which the use of the decision-making structure is discussed. Discussion and agreement on the use of processes and their improvement is always a wise investment of time, if conducted with clear purposes in mind. It is a task of no small political significance.

Choosing and controlling the agencies

Having put the work of the department into a strategic framework, the committee can now consider which agencies are most suitable to carry out the work and, in particular, its links with the operation of its associated services. The very existence of a directly provided service implies that the council believes in its own capacity to provide the service directly as the best way of implementing its current *directions* — but that assumes the council has thought out the options! Councillors are frequently involved in what is being done by a service, both as members of the relevant committee and as constituency representatives. But the next step in the organised progression from corporate *directions* through committee strategy to service delivery must be democratic control of the whole of the work being carried out.

Assuming that the committee has articulated a strategy for achieving the council's *directions*, there are two important questions to be considered now:

▽ How can the committee avoid unwanted side effects from the way the achievements it seeks are being gained?

▽ How can the committee so organise its control that the minimum obstruction is placed in the way of the line management responsible for the achievements?

A third question — How does the committee maintain an economical and efficient service organization? — is discussed in the next chapter.

These questions assume objectives which may be in conflict with each other . . . yet both objectives are valid. There is the objective of achieving the council's *directions* efficiently and the objective of minimising public displeasure about the way in which the work is done. The political cost of economical and efficient achievement may be too high if the consequential disturbance to people's lives is very great. The precise line of a proposed road scheme may be the very best that civil engineers can produce under the committee's strategy for achieving the council's *direction* about improving ease of movement to and from a certain area. But the effect on local residents, or on the natural environment, may be such that a variation has to be paid for. The nuisance of the road works themselves may require a balance to be struck between speed of progress and the efficient length of the working day or week. So we are soon at the level of overwhelming detail if adequate control arrangements are not made.

If the committee allows its time to be hijacked by operational detail (a subject to which we return, in greater detail (!), on p. 61), it is almost bound to become little more than a supporters' club, disputing about minor details, working for more resources and warding off interference from what it sees as busybodies, like 'the personnel sub-committee with its ideas on recruitment'. On the other hand, if the committee is divorced from the day-to-day activities and operational problems faced by its departments it may make unrealistic demands, or leave the departments without guidance in the midst of public controversy; hence, the importance of monitoring performance.

Controlling the in-house services

The balance between the two competing objectives is very relevant to the choice of agency. The in-house, directly controlled service may — or may not — be more economical than an outside contractor but it ought to be more responsive to political sensitivities in the methods it adopts. These services are an inheritance — a set of valuable assets representing considerable public investment over many years. They have developed individual characteristics, professional standards and — of increasing significance — links with individual government departments as service-related issues appear more and more as part of the national political agenda. They each have an individual momentum of their own which often defies strong local council *directions*.

The services affect the life of every citizen. They cannot be ignored. Can they be put in their place? How can the council control its services so that they are concentrated on achieving its objectives? How can the council help the services to operate effectively? How can the council prevent the services from becoming ends in themselves instead of its directly provided means to currently authorised ends? How can the council weigh the effectiveness of its services against that of alternative agencies?

Without the discipline outlined in Chapter 4 and the operationally based *directions* which are the outcome, it will be difficult to answer these questions. With the *directions* as a basis, the position of each service can be more clearly determined. The *directions* concerned with *targets* to be attacked in the local community (e.g. urban regeneration) should prompt a variety of organisational responses. The council's directly provided services will rarely have a monopoly of appropriate responses to priority needs. The *directions* concerned with finance will encourage optimum use by committees of the defined resources which the council has allocated. No longer is the financial imperative of a service committee limited to fighting other services for a greater share of fictitiously open-ended resources. Through *directions* concerned with *operating values*, the council and its committees can begin to control the ways in which the services operate, while conferring a proper freedom for initiative.

Unless the committee undertakes a systematic review of the whole of 'its' departments' work and the relationship of that work to the council's current objectives, the likelihood is that large portions of the council's directly employed organisation will never come under its effective jurisdiction, nor will it be possible to make a sound judgment about choice of agency. Indeed, many parts will already have slipped away unnoticed, for example:

▽   Although the council is the employer, its rates of pay and conditions of service are almost entirely settled by national arrangements which were originally optional but now (by weight of industrial relations or by law) are effectively removed from the council's control. There goes the largest single item of expenditure for a start!

▽   Operational land and buildings are largely taken for granted, with options for better usage getting lost in internal rivalries and lack of clear political commitment. The subject is dealt with in greater detail in *Our Heritage*, a report by a working group on behalf of the RIBA, RICS, CIPFA and SOLACE in 1986, and in a recent Audit Commission Report (February 1988). Premises-related costs (including some pay) are likely to account for over 20% of expenditure.

▽   Activities which are not politically significant will just keep going. The employees involved will rarely volunteer the redundancy of their work and members can only determine the lack of polical priority by reviewing all activities against a set of *directions* and consequential strategies. Based on experience, it would not be unreasonable to suggest that a 20% redirection of resources is usually possible after such an exercise. Why does it take the researches of an Audit Commission or the use of consultants to expose options which local processes have unquestioningly accepted?

Of course, a very strong reason for not pursuing a systematic review of all of a service committee's responsibilities may be an understandable dislike of even more detail to cope with. If management information is to be relevant to members' needs, the sorting out of each committee's responsibilities into manageable units, leading to meaningful comparisons of budgetary and other 'input' information with 'output' and 'impact on the problem' information for each unit, will initially require a considerable effort and throw up a lot of difficult issues requiring member involvement in the process. Delegation by the full committee to formal sub-committees or, better still, informal working groups is certainly a useful option, and preferable to the use of the committee's formal processes for this consequential, though important, supervision.

By initiating its own practical strategy for achieving the corporate *directions* and positively choosing appropriate agencies to deliver the results, the committee will have taken a major step in operational control, without having to wade through recurring detail. It will be able to keep in touch with reality by setting key *targets* for achievement and monitoring the results (Chapter 9). It will be able to rely on the council's advance commitment of resources to work out its strategy and to revise both the strategy, and its advice on future resources needed, in the light of actual achievements. In the next chapter we look at the consequences of this approach for departmental structures and individual jobs. This is all in great contrast to a committee which, without the backing of corporate *directions* and commitments, inherits a department with well-defined ways of working, an established and apparently unalterable range of activities, and a traditional career ladder, with the 'tail' of implementation wagging the 'dog' of democratic choice. Yet what can a committee of part-time lay people do to control such a department if its formal agenda is geared only to the day-to-day issues? Such a department is, with some justification, likely to have a cynical resignation to random operational interference by the committee and will therefore keep up elaborate defences against member involvement in anything of major operational importance. If this does not succeed, the managers may well give up the struggle for managerial consistency in the face of random detailed decisions and leave the committee 'to get on with it'. Certainly it will be selfishly defensive about the use of other agencies. Such attitudes weaken still further the ability of the councillors to achieve cost-effective control at a strategic level, and so the cycle of non-*direction* constantly worsens. Perhaps it is fortunate that in such situations the professional ethics and inherited traditions of the department will give some consistency of background to service delivery at the 'sharp end' — in a school, or a residential hostel — where the village games of the council's 'top' organisation are seen to have little relevance.

Distancing the committee from operational detail

In the battle against domination by the detail of in-house service management, the extent to which a committee divests itself of day-to-day control should obviously be related to the effectiveness of the control systems it has been able to develop and establish. Increasingly, some councils are finding it valuable to distance line management from their collective processes. Most councils, for example, will have had to consider radical changes in the control and management of their direct labour organisations, as a result of legislative requirements to become competitive. If the level of efficiency required by competitiveness could only be met by substantial delegation to line management but without loss of important democratic values, how many other activities would benefit from similar treatment?

At one extreme of political disengagement from operational line management is the 'contracting out' of the activity to another organisation. This is not 'privatisation', where the council's power to provide a service is removed. In 'contracting out', the nature and range of the service is still determined by the council, but the management of service delivery is contracted to an external agent, with or without conditions about working methods. If a major political objective is to be able to intervene in detailed arrangements, or to provide the service in a way which is impossible except through the council's own directly provided organisation, or to set a unique standard as employer of the service employees, then contracting out will not be a voluntary option. But where it brings advantages of less cost, more specialised expertise or well-organised innovation, then the unquestioning acceptance of the existing 'in-house' arrangements is a dereliction of duty.

The use of another authority's computer and related expertise, for example, or its highly specialist and successful financial forecasting; the granting of an agency to another public authority on terms of mutual benefit; special arrangements with neighbouring authorities for the most cost-effective service delivery near an operationally difficult boundary; these are examples of well-established but limited practices of disengagement by making good use of the services of another local authority.

Another disengagement device, for which the legal requirements are complex, is the creation of a company in which the authority is the major shareholder or, in some other way, the principal beneficiary. This device is used in West Germany where, for example, electricity and water supplies are provided by limited companies with their own line management, but where *direction* is given by the local authorities of the area, who are the main shareholders.

Enterprises run by a joint committee, e.g. a purchasing consortium, tend to permit freedom of management because the accumulated heap of local rules, safeguards and other reactions to individual circumstances over many years in each participating authority have no automatic application to the management of the joint enterprise and councillors in each participating authority do not seem to feel the same immediate responsibility for detail that so often applies to 'in-house' work.

Commercial businesses operating in widely distributed activities like cleaning have replaced in-house arrangements in many authorities. The very existence of the option has often improved the efficiency of the in-house arrangements and it is a reflection on the dynamism of local authorities in controlling their organisations that legislation has been the moving force in identifying more efficient means rather than the searching perception of the individual local authorities.

Many authorities are now establishing cost-centre disciplines on all their bureaucratic and professional support functions to establish a realistic choice for the service managers in buying, for example, their legal advice 'in-house' or from a firm of solicitors. Legislation is now proposed which will extend this approach compulsorily to several traditional 'in-house' services, and there is growing experience in the management of what, for many authorities, is a new kind of operational relationship.

Coping with the curse of detail

Just as the council cannot hope to control its organisation by constantly asking questions about the value of each individual job and employee — important though they all are — so it cannot hope to cope directly with the equally important detail of individual service delivery. Good aggregated management information is the appropriate diet for the most senior democratic processes, unless the circumstances are very exceptional, and other processes can be created to ensure critical sensitivity. These and good 'staff' support from employees and sub-committees should enable the committees to be sufficiently aware of day-to-day activities and operational problems, so that unrealistic demands are avoided and guidance or support can be given in the midst of public controversy.

Yet, however good the discipline of practical *direction*-setting and the monitoring of achievement, some detailed issues of implementation will have to have attention, but the extent to which the committee is troubled will be a test of the soundness and clarity of the council's and the committee's work in the *directions* and strategy they have created. If the collective decisions of the members are sound and clear, it will usually be weakness of management or inadequate 'staff' work which causes the frequent reference back of operational details.

Consideration of detail in committee is not in the interests of democratic control. It reduces the time and energy available to reach the key decisions which enable the complex employee structure to be held accountable. It focuses excessive attention on disputes, exceptions and special cases. It encourages policy making by stealth and it weakens sound line management. Indeed, in the absence of a genuinely agreed and achievable overall strategy, the only control the members have is over the details which happen to appear on their particular committee agendas. It is not unknown for the extremely busy education committee never to have considered the relevance of the current curricula or the considerable waste of resources involved in under-used secondary schools. The sheer weight of individual issues, undoubtedly important to some, drive out any opportunity for the committee to seize major initiatives.

Twenty years ago, the Maud Committee was very scathing in its criticism of the local authority obsession with detail in their committee work, but the feature is of such long standing that the reasons which make it so must be identified and dealt with if the detail is to be put in its place. We suggest three principal reasons for the excessive dominance of detail:

▽   specialist professionalism;
▽   the absence of performance measures;
▽   pressures from constituents.

Specialist professionalism

The first is the inability of a lay council, now with a rapid turnover of membership, to grasp the initiative in relation to highly complex, long developed, professionalised services about which the only organised management information is that which supports the series of ad hoc items appearing on the committee's agendas. Present practice stems back through days when the aldermanic system provided a longer collective memory in the council to the very early days when local leaders were both the organisers and the planners of the services' origins and purposes. The alderman who gave the borough its first public park in 1863, and became first chairman of its parks committee, was able to cope with incidental detail because he helped to create the relevant *directions*, commitments and strategy (though he might not have recognised those terms). In the actual case we have in mind, no parks superintendent was appointed for many years — the chairman saw to it that the committee's intentions were carried out! The very first services of modern local authorities were conceived after careful and deep preparation of the evidence necessary to secure a private Act of Parliament amidst the squalor of early nineteenth-century urbanisation, and the initial promoters were themselves often the foremost experts in their locality on the technical requirements of the remedies needed. The councillor of today is, by contrast, usually unfamiliar with the long history, the structure and even the wide-ranging tasks of large parts of the services for which the council is responsible. The services exist as established background to current political concerns rather than as resources to be directed. The sheer weight of the well-established services prevents control even by those councillors deeply involved in the informal processes which lie behind the formal agendas, if the initiative for comprehending the services' activities is unaided by 'top down' processes and relevant 'staff' work. The ongoing requirements of the service for formal committee and council approval to detailed adaptation or development provide the only opportunities available for giving *direction* in a practical way. To delegate detailed decision-making to officers when the council's systems and processes give inadequate opportunities for establishing basic purpose or assessing achievement would remove almost any opportunity for control or influence. We have tried to meet this reason by suggesting the *direction*-setting and forward commitment processes of the council and the strategy-making function of the committee.

The absence of performance measures

The second reason for the prevalence of detailed agenda is the absence of adequate performance measures with which the councillors can monitor the achievements of a service. The need to seek frequent detailed authorisation from a committee puts different parts of the service randomly under scrutiny and allows members to express criticisms or support. It gives them a variety of opportunities to influence what is going on. The current development of performance measures and monitoring systems is dealt with in Chapter 9.

Pressures from constituents

The third reason is the need for individual councillors to be able to answer questions or take up complaints and concerns as they occur in their local divisions or wards. If there is no other process provided to meet this need then, as with the two previous reasons, the process which is available will be put under pressure. Most local complaints and concerns can be dealt with more quickly and effectively than by going to a committee by direct contact with the line manager involved. Much local trouble can be forestalled by genuine consultation before some major service initiative disrupts local people's lives. The committee's agendas and minutes are not very efficient either as a news bulletin or as an internal departmental management process.

It is, therefore, not sufficent to exhort councillors to rid themselves of detail in their formal meetings. These three and any other reasons which promote detail in committee must be dealt with first.

Quite apart from the defeat of democratic control, the clutter of detail in a committee is also bad news for good line managers, again for three principal reasons:

▽   diffusion of executive responsibility;
▽   confusion of basic directions;
▽   remoteness from the action.

Diffusion of executive responsibility

The line of management from the council, through the committee and the chief officer to the direct deliverers of the service to the public is thrown into confusion when some individual detail is said, by someone apparently remote from the action bureaucrat, to require formal approval or because it is the subject of a complaint. Holding the appropriate line manager responsible for achievement is impossible if the interference and delay of the committee process has effectively transferred that responsibility to the committee. Not only that, but the detached decision will have to be observed in future similar situations until it is formally rescinded and will act as a precedent no matter how inappropriate it becomes. The more widespread the committee's detailed interference, the worse the line management's discipline and purposefulness becomes. In one authority, a technically correct, but no longer politically justifiable, decision made by counter staff in the Housing Department in 1969 was accurately traced back to a detailed council decision of 1931.

Confusion of basic *directions*

Secondly, there is the risk of detailed decisions confusing the clarity and authority of whatever council *direction* and committee strategy there may be in the minds of those employed to carry them out. Decisions in committee can be motivated by many other reasons than single-minded commitment to the practical results sought by the council, more particularly when the detail appears so insignificant that not very much seems at stake in the immediate practical consequences. Compromise on one issue to match a compromise on another; special pleading by an influential member; remoteness of many of the members from the practical consequences — these and many other factors can cause a detailed decision to be made which makes the operational employees wonder whether their understanding of the purpose of their work is correct. In the absence of clear council *directions* the permanent employees inevitably become the custodians of consistency; the danger is that the councillors are reduced to the role of critics of the apparently independent services.

Remoteness from the action

Thirdly, the physical and cultural remoteness of the county or town hall from the action can make it difficult, if not impossible, for the arguments in favour of a particular operational initiative to be understood by a committee, with the result that novel, practical ideas for solving problems fail to impress and the council's services become dated and unadventurous. The lowest common denominator of lay agreement reinforces purposelessness.

In Chapter 4 we considered a scheme of delegation complementary to the council's *directions* and so enabling their creative and enterprising implementation. Without such a scheme and *directions*, it is difficult to see how, for example, decentralisation by a local authority can work. It is then almost inevitable that detail will be forced to rise to the highest possible level for determination and thus defeat the intended benefit of really local sensitivity.

A reduction to a minimum of the clutter of non-strategic detail from a committee's agenda is essential if it is to be able to exercise real control on behalf of the council. The extent of delegation which is desirable will vary with the degree of mutual trust and the clarity and extent of the *directions* which the council has been able to frame. At committee level, similarly, the scale of delegation to sub-committees and officials should be worked out in relationship with the committee's ability to control the factors which it considers are important.

The prime responsibility, as always, is with the councillors to ensure that their time is properly used. Instead of encouraging operational detail and individual 'policy' matters to appear on their committee agendas by uncomplainingly accepting as appropriate for their decision whatever items happen to appear, committee members should rigorously question the value which their deliberations will add to the decisions reached; and then set that value against the administrative cost, the delay in implementation, the confusion of line management responsibility, and the diversionary clutter which consideration of unworthy items involves. The irony of the situation is that the traditional executive committee actually prevents members from exercising effective democratic control, even though the desire for it is the spur which keeps it going.

Questions

▲   1. *Taking the operational strategy you identified when dealing with Question 1 of Chapter 1 on page 14, where is this authoritatively set down? What role did the committees play in the creation of this strategy? How does the strategy influence the way the council deals with ad hoc items for decision?*

▲   2. *How are the agencies for carrying out this strategy selected and chosen? What checks are there to show that they live up to the reasons for their choice? What is the purpose of your using 'in-house' services? Can your reasons be clearly validated?*

▲   3. *Collect the year's agendas for the committee mainly concerned with the issue you identified when dealing with Question 1 of Chapter 1 on page 14. Applying the ideas in this chapter, identify which items ought not to have come to committee. What should have been included, but wasn't?*

▲   4. *Take the* directions *of the council which you worked out when tackling the questions at the end of Chapter 4 on page 42, and work out ways of implementing them without making use of the council's own service organisations.*

▲   5. *The chapter argues, on page 59, that many parts of the committee's service organisation will have slipped away unnoticed from its control. Consider the activities for which the committee you identified in Question 3 is responsible. Identify what has 'slipped away unnoticed'. Why?*

7 Managing departmental organisation

Creating a sense of direction for the organisation requires people at the top (councillors and senior employees) to be co-directors of the whole business of governing, not just barons protecting their own corners. Pre-occupation by 'classic' professional departments (and other associated committees) with their particular services disables the organisation from evolving as an integrated whole. Time and attention at senior levels in the organisation should be focused more 'upwards' and 'outwards' than 'downwards' and 'inwards'.

The organisation should be shaped around its 'core' businesses (housing, education, the local economy, etc.) with those accountable for them together taking the lead role as the 'core' of top management. Those directors should direct. Supporters (finance, personnel, etc.) should support. Contractors (property, transport, etc.) should contract. The different contributions and relationship required of each should be explicitly defined and agreed — and their interdependence and performance jointly reviewed.

Departmental functions versus cross-departmental objectives

In the last chapter we explored the role of members in converting the broad *directions* of the council into practical strategies for achieving results — the first intermediate level of line management between the council and the most junior employee. In this chapter we look at some of the major considerations involved in the organisation of all the intermediate levels of management created by the council through the hiring of employees, based on the inevitable bureaucratic model of a descending hierarchy of authority from the council — the departmental organisation. It is therefore especially concerned with 'top-down' direction — as against 'bottom-up' pressures. The latter are important but are often channelled by the history and ambitions of professional departments into the typically vertical segmentation of local authority structures, whose functions are based on definitions of social problems in earlier times or on professionally defined specialist advice. The actual subjects of the council's broad-brush concerns will frequently run horizontally across these departments, e.g. economic development, environmental protection, the elderly, value for money. See Fig. 5. As the hitherto local initiatives mature into national services provided by national professions, the challenge is to create an organisation capable of dealing with current local problems on the initiative of the council, despite the confused lines of central and local responsibility for and the different professional outlooks of the traditional 'services', and the difficulty of managing complex service organisations through outdated processes of detailed executive decision-making.

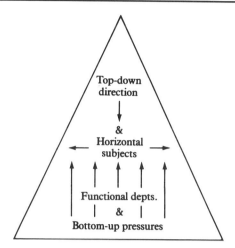

Figure 5. Is there a mismatch?

The weakest feature of local authorities is the one where they should be most strong, viz. in giving direction and reviewing performance to fulfil their purpose in the local community. Conversely, their strongest feature is the solidarity and separateness of their departmental-based structures. In many authorities the drive is almost entirely bottom-up, not top-down, is focused on departmental rather than the council's ambitions, and deals poorly with across-the-board 'horizontal' issues. At best, the respective sectional contributions are co-ordinated rather than integrated. In effect, the departmental *tail* wags the corporate *dog*. But departments are really only a means to an end. They are groupings of hired skills, convenient for management, training and career development, and organised so as to deliver specific results. But they have often become professional hierarchies which, with national migration of employees across them and the formation of supportive professional societies at national level, are not unnaturally seen from an employee point of view as a permanent place of work for the pursuit of their careers, with the employing local authority providing a background of local colour. These departments have served local government well and with great integrity, taking their responsibilities to their professions and the public very seriously — until recently being professionals first and managers second. The need to move from 'professional responsibility' to 'managerial accountability' is now an acknowledged idea whose time has come. Yet, as we have argued earlier in Chapter 5, senior employees should not only be accountable for their effectiveness professionally and managerially, but also for their contribution as corporate 'staff' officers serving the authority as a whole (which after all is their employer) and not just 'their' department. If the council is concerned about changing local problems, the heads of those departments are not paid to operate in isolation (however well) but together to develop, recommend and review integrated policies and programmes which help to create and to give effect to the *directions* of the council.

Directions first, management and implementation afterwards

Thus we must expect departments themselves to exhibit individually a loyalty to

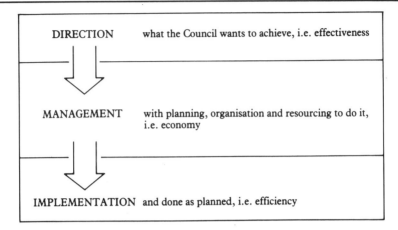

Figure 6. Different kinds of activity

the same three levels of contribution that must also be made collectively within the authority as a whole (see Fig. 6).

Our concern is primarily with direction and the conversion of the council's *directions* into action. Management and implementation are consequential items — vital obviously, but flowing from the main purpose. Whatever 'line management arrangements' the authority adopts, they must reflect not only good management theory and practice, but the whole spirit of what the council is trying to do through the *directions* it gives as to:

▽   *targets* for attack;
▽   *financing*;
▽   *operating values* (see Chapter 4).

We use the term 'line management arrangements' to cover:

▽   structures (the collection of jobs into departments and family trees);
▽   processes (for identifying needs, planning, budgeting, control, evaluation, communication etc.);
▽   performance management (self-criticism, collective appraisal, internal and external promotion of results etc.).

How all these are shaped and integrated will depend not only on the directions in which the council wants to go (Chapter 4) but also on the concerns it addresses from time to time as to its continued organisational health and vitality (Chapter 1).

As to the question of direction:

▽   if the council is determined to make a major push on, say, economic development, it may:
      — appoint a separate accountable officer with a free-standing department, or
      — allocate the task to a central corporate unit, or
      — determine an authority-wide master plan to which several departments must contribute, with an accountability on them to integrate their work across the matrix,
      — . . . or whatever.

▽   If the council is unhappy because its needs for dynamic property management, investment and the use of its land and buildings as a corporate resource are not being best met, it may:
— combine all property-related departments, or
— appoint a multi-disciplinary steering group, or
— bring in outside expertise, or
— undertake systematic reviews of large slices of the property portfolio, or
— invest in relevant training across all departments,
— . . . or whatever.

As to its organisational health, for example:

▽   if the council feels it has lost creative vitality in its staff, there are several options for improvement, such as:
— giving greater freedom to act (subject to basic controls being in place), or
— loosening its chain of command over detail, or
— investing in training and career development, or
— zig-zagging staff through different departments,
— . . . or whatever.
▽   if it feels it needs to tighten its financial and other controls it may, conversely:
— limit some freedoms, or
— tighten its command chain, or
— keep staff more strictly focused on what they are trained to do,
— . . . or whatever.

Thus, the council's targets for attack, and its philosophies on financing and operations, will all interact to inform the shape and character of the way it organises its departments.

Grouping the work

Over the years, some councils have grouped functions to secure a movement away from too narrow and compartmentalised a focus which accentuates vertical professional hierarchies and towards a more horizontal subject focus, as Fig. 7 demonstrates. The possible permutations are almost endless and these indications of how some groupings may be identified are illustrative only. There are many questions to be asked and trade-offs to be made. Are the different pulls of 'environmental protection' and 'public access to the countryside' best accommodated in a particular authority by combining the two and forcing their reconciliation that way, or are they best kept at arms' length with a deliberate 'separation of powers', in order to keep their respective voices and consciences clear, with integration achieved by the councillors after hearing both sides? In one seaside town the preservation and exploitation of its natural assets may both be as one, but in another there may be much potential conflict between the two. It will be evident that the answer by no means lies solely with decisions about structure — so much depends upon the way in which the council is able to organise its thinking, prioritising, resource allocation and arbitration processes and to rely on its people. This underlines our theme that the most critical elements of all the council's work are the need to equip itself and all its staff with clear *directions* whose achievement is carefully monitored, and to evolve an organisation which is responsive, adaptive and alive to the need to reshape itself creatively in ways which will best make those *directions* happen.

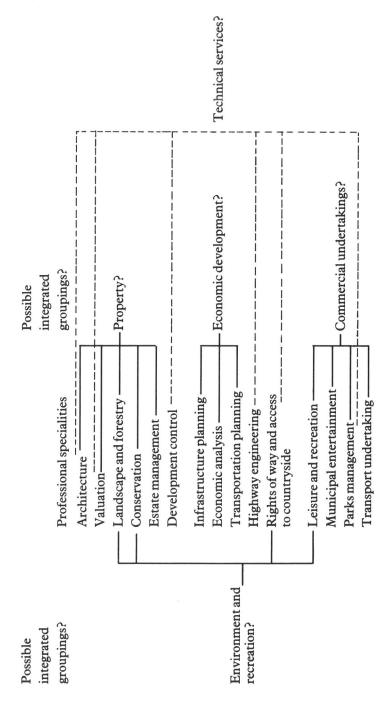

Figure 7. Possible structural groupings

But we are not saying that traditional structures are wrong per se. If there are clear *directions*, good people, effective collaboration between departments and purposeful planning, control and review mechanisms, then almost any structure can be made to work. Having said that, however, all our experience tells us that the longevity and tradition of some of the classic professional structures are barriers to change. Often as not, the sort of reorganised groupings illustrated in Fig. 7 are brought about by councillors themselves, despairing at departmental compartmentalism or conflict, or responding to the opportunity presented by a retiring chief officer. Occasionally, and often with outside consultancy help, such an initiative has sensibly led to a comprehensive review of the whole controlling structure of the organisation and in this chapter we draw in large measure from experience of these 'whole organisation' reviews over the past decade.

Conducting an organisational review; integrity of purpose

In setting about such a 'review', it is fundamental that its purpose should be owned by the councillors and seen, not as something which is being 'done to' the employee or councillor organisation, but 'done for' the councillors to enable them to be more effective through their employees. Hence, long before any review begins to grapple with the content, it must first gain consent as to how it is to be organised as a process. The aim should be to get the commitment and trust of councillors (of all party groups and persuasions) that it is genuinely being undertaken to improve the council's capability to fulfil its Widdicombe *raison d'être* of being a vital and participative part of the democratic process of self-government charged with sensitive service delivery.

Establishing the integrity of the purpose behind organisational review in this way is vital. First, because it demonstrates that it is about better government by the council, and thereby relegates any suspicions that 'it's a so-called efficiency review really designed to cut back resources' or 'a ploy to uncover yet more needs and justify more resources' or 'a plot to give more power to a select few'.

Secondly, because it enables the key issues of concern to be neutrally tabled by councillors and employees alike — 'poor staff morale', 'underinvestment in school building maintenance', 'need for middle-management training', 'a crippling lack of political inter-party collaboration on common issues', 'conflict between the policy committee and service committees', 'too many meetings and too much paper', 'no feedback on whether we are achieving what we set out to', 'no clear guidance or consistency from the councillors', etc.

Thirdly, because it requires councillors to address what they really are in business for and to state their own objectives, priorities and perceptions about where they are now, compared to where they want to be — thereby starting the process of identifying *directions*. After all, without this, how is it going to be possible to give an organisational review any sensible steer? Neither the organisation nor the review are worthwhile ends in themselves.

But, of course, this sort of review should be a continuous process of self-examination as a way of life rather than root and branch disturbance — necessary as that may be from time to time. Effective continuous review must largely depend on the capacity for internal self-examination by the officers and clarity of purpose by the councillors. Hence an open, inquiring attitude to organisation is needed, not one which is hell-bent on preserving the *status quo* and defending existing resource patterns. And that depends on the quality of the top people

— *all* the top people — chief officers, chief executive and councillors, bonded at the very least by an unshaken belief in the Widdicombe attributes — in the permanent *purposes* of local government more than the current *means*.

Top jobs are about supporting the council

A major inhibition to all this is the excessive 'bottom-up' rather than 'top-down' orientation of local authority top people, councillors and employees alike. The perspective of both is so often derived from the particular professional or sectional 'box' in which they happened to start their local authority work. As they move up through the organisation and become chairmen or chief officers, their view is often still departmentally or committee based and, of course, powerful liaisons develop between chairmen and their chief officers which reinforce this. In the absence of effective corporate processes, it is the only way to survive because concessions to a wider perspective will be seen as signs of weakness, both by the service people they seek to lead and by the other committee and departmental leaders caught in the same trap.

But top jobs are different in kind, not more of the same — or should be; yet many top job holders rarely see their jobs as being more than about the downwards business of continuing to run a particular department or committee. We would argue that at the top, jobs should be much less about that (though they remain accountable and require appropriate assistance for it) and much more about the contribution they should make upwards to the authority as a whole, sideways towards their colleague top job holders and outwards in understanding and influencing the external world and promoting the authority's views and achievements (Fig. 8).

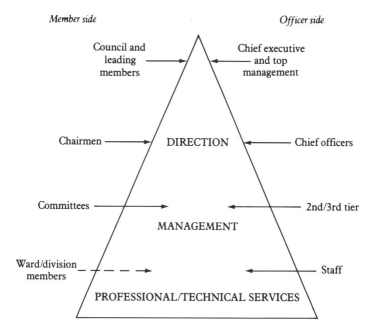

Figure 8. Making the right level of contribution

```
                          ┌─────────────────┐
                          │ Upwards ?%      │
                          │ ─ Help council  │
                          │   establish and │
                          │   review overall│
                          │   directions and│
                          │   offer individual│
                          │   policy        │
                          │   contributions │
                          └─────────────────┘

┌─────────────────┐  ┌─────────────────┐  ┌─────────────────┐
│ Sideways ?%     │  │ Selfwards ?%    │  │ Outwards ?%     │
│ ─ Help resolve  │  │ ─ Keep up-to-date│  │ ─ Understand    │
│   organisation- │  │ ─ Political/    │  │   and influence │
│   wide issues and│  │   professional/ │  │   externally: listen│
│   develop common│  │   technical     │  │   and sell to   │
│   systems       │  │   contacts      │  │   customers,    │
│ ─ Collaborate and│  │ ─ Develop own   │  │   public local/ │
│   integrate with│  │   capabilities and│  │   national bodies│
│   other parts of the│  │   growth    │  │                 │
│   organisation  │  │                 │  │                 │
└─────────────────┘  └─────────────────┘  └─────────────────┘

                          ┌─────────────────┐
                          │ Downwards ?%    │
                          │ ─ Deliver       │
                          │   department's  │
                          │   operational   │
                          │   results       │
                          │ ─ Direct, control│
                          │   and motivate  │
                          │   staff         │
                          └─────────────────┘
```

Figure 9. Top jobs: Their different contributions to overall organisational effectiveness

Figure 9 is a useful and simple device that has been powerfully employed to stimulate chairmen and chief officers to think about their different roles and the effort they put into each of them. Assess what proportion of your time and that of your equivalent chairman/chief officer is spent in each of the five boxes. A common (and worrying) distribution of time reported back to us would be as illustrated in Fig. 10.

Typically, too little time is spent on the upwards and sideways aspects of the job as a co-director of the whole business of the council. Of the 'outwards' and 'selfwards' aspects, too little time is spent on promotion of the authority generally or on development of individual capabilities — the pre-occupation being much more with professional networks and internal problems to do with the department.

The connection between this analysis and the shaping of departments accord-

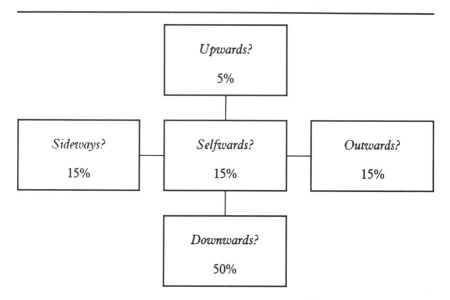

Figure 10. Top jobs: the usual distribution of time and effort

ing to the changing needs of the organisation will be obvious. Those needs, whether because of increasing numbers of 'horizontal' issues or because of the need to give pre-eminence to general integrated managerial direction over pure professional hierarchies, will mean that departmental directors will need to see their jobs as delivering a corporate contribution to the whole rather than performing a discrete professional service. If we were to define the job of a 'department' (and, by extension, that of the job of its directors) this should help crystallise performance requirements in meeting its real purpose for being there as distinct from the much narrower function of providing a particular and established means of public service, however important that means may be.

Accept, for the moment, the generic definition in Fig. 11 and make a judgment about how well a given department (and its director) is performing under each heading. Would you mark your chosen department as making a high (H), medium (M), or low (L) contribution in each case?

It will be seen that this echoes, at departmental level, the distinction made earlier between supporting the concept of local government as a purpose and recognising the local authority as a means. The 'job description' is deliberately drafted to reflect the primary responsibility of the department to support the council's purposes and only secondarily to provide the means of fulfilment.

What departments, why, and comprising whom?

Our aim thus far has been to establish the notion that departments, their direction and their directors are there to support the council and service the whole organisation by participation in the setting and achievement of its *directions*. But how many departments should there be, and of what sort? The easy answer is 'whatever is appropriate to the achievement of the council's *directions*, its strengths and weaknesses at any given time; in particular its ability to lead, control and motivate those departments as the main components of its organisation'.

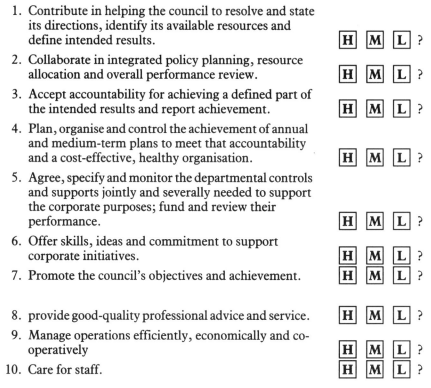

1. Contribute in helping the council to resolve and state
   its directions, identify its available resources and
   define intended results.   H   M   L   ?

2. Collaborate in integrated policy planning, resource
   allocation and overall performance review.   H   M   L   ?

3. Accept accountability for achieving a defined part of
   the intended results and report achievement.   H   M   L   ?

4. Plan, organise and control the achievement of annual
   and medium-term plans to meet that accountability
   and a cost-effective, healthy organisation.   H   M   L   ?

5. Agree, specify and monitor the departmental controls
   and supports jointly and severally needed to support
   the corporate purposes; fund and review their
   performance.   H   M   L   ?

6. Offer skills, ideas and commitment to support
   corporate initiatives.   H   M   L   ?

7. Promote the council's objectives and achievement.   H   M   L   ?

8. provide good-quality professional advice and service. H   M   L   ?

9. Manage operations efficiently, economically and co-
   operatively   H   M   L   ?

10. Care for staff.   H   M   L   ?

Figure 11. The job of a department . . . in support of the council's purposes

Obviously, this isn't good enough, though no single blueprint can ever be prescribed. We therefore need to establish some principles by which to test our existing management arrangements and to act as a framework for their adaptation over time. Remember, the phrase is 'management arrangements', not just departmental structures of jobs, because the linking processes of needs evaluation, planning, control and review, and the skills, attitudes and motivation of its recruited people are also very important.

Let us pretend that none of the current organisation existed — none of its departments, jobs or people — councillor or employee. We have a clean sheet of paper and the task is to design an organisation from scratch to deliver all current services and meet obvious local priorities.

Naturally one would want to start by gathering around oneself a band of good people to work collaboratively at the problem and then divide up responsibilities according to skills, with individuals accountable for certain chunks of the business.

Let us make this fancy a little more practical. The starting point in a local authority must be for an appropriate, credible and persuasive group of elected members to take ownership of their collective accountability: to determine precisely what the authority is there to achieve in their particular locality and what key results areas they would feel it necessary to give, as jobs, to individuals to be accountable for. In other words, they would divide up the work and set up the organisation. Let's assume they came up initially with vague *targets* for attack such as 'a clean and attractive natural and built environment', 'an economical infrastructure of communications, energy and waste disposal', 'opportunity for gainful employment for all', 'education and experience to provide economically and spiritually satisfying lives for all' and so forth. To each of the allotted individuals, the following proposition would then be put: 'here's your brief, go away and tell us how you propose to get the results we want; say what precisely you will achieve over what timescale, at what cost and with what return, together with your plan for organising and controlling what you do and the people you employ (whether from inside or outside) and tell us what resources you will need for the next three or four years within such a total limit — also if that limit is unrealistic, in which case we may have to think again'.

Now, along the way, they will need to take into account any preferences the council has about financing and working practices, e.g. borrowing, charges, contracting out, part-time employment etc., so that these flow through into the nature of the organisation they construct.

Of course a variety of solutions may well emerge, some of a completely different character from others and not necessarily the worse for that. After all, the solutions should fit the character of the work to be done, and the client groups to be served, rather than conform to some stereotype. The culture and organisation for dealing with the needs of the elderly on the one hand, and the dangers of fire on the other, will obviously be very different. Without doubt, though, an issue for consideration when all their initial propositions for their own organisations are collected together, is what consistency should there be? Not for its own sake, but where it matters in the interest of synergy, control or economy of scale.

The point about carrying out such a hypothetical exercise is not necessarily to set about a major review, as such, but to free thinking as to the ways things might be different. There are many potentially different ways of organising other than by the traditional departmental hierarchies.

Of course, nothing is forever. The pace of social, democratic and economic changes in the local community has never been quicker. The objectives for which those arrangements may be designed may well be met quite quickly. The accountable committee, working group, joint officer/member team, inter-departmental working party, or whatever it was that was charged with designing the organisation and which was appropriate to see it into this world, may not be the appropriate body to maintain it. Similarly, subordinate concerns, such as lack of staff creativity or of adequate control mechanisms, and which might have added an extra reason for an authority deciding to organise in a particular way, should not last for long if they are purposefully tackled, and hence the management arrangements can be reshaped as time goes by. An organisation's management arrangements must be continually on the move to meet new stimuli, and to use and change its resources of skills more effectively.

Line, corporate support and contracted jobs

Let us look at this question of resources more closely. In a 'clean sheet' operation, some radically different choices may come forward by contrast with current forms of delivery. Laying aside all questions of political dogma, it might prove very tempting to provide some services entirely on a sub-contracted basis, with someone else bearing the continuing cost and worry of capital investment and staff employment — but this would require very strict specification of the requirements for the contracted service, performance review, guarantees of style and behaviour etc. Suffice it to say there are ways of providing services other than in-house.

In the field of 'support services', such as law, personnel, property and finance, here again it is perfectly possible to contract out to commercial firms, and especially for peak or very unusual work. Insofar as these sorts of services are provided internally, they need to be deployed to best effect as a corporate resource in the service of the authority as a whole, and of its line, operational activities in particular, with clear performance specifications being set and met as though they were provided by an external contractor.

Let us extend the notion of a 'corporate resource' to all the other 'departments' of the authority. We have already argued in Chapter 5 that there is a key 'staff' role to be played in and by all departments, so let us gather all those staff together (say the top 15%) and recognise them, not as an elite but as a network of colleagues whose development, synergy and commitment it will be essential to engage if the authority is to flourish. Such a 'corporate resource' of staff will cut across all departments, and its development and commitment should be a key concern of the chief executive.

The tests of organisational design

With all these thoughts in mind, we come at last to the issue of departments and how they might be organised. Having decided what you want to do (*directions*), the practical philosophy to be followed (*financing* and *operating values*) and the people to be responsible for performance (accountability and synergy), it is clear that:

∇   the most critical resource is the top people, so their recruitment, motivation, development and planned succession is critical;
∇   there needs to be constant organisational evolution;
∇   the 'organisation' must be understood as much more than structure alone, being also about processes, people and performance;
∇   the council's management arrangements must be informed by its declared *directions* and philosophies;
∇   departmental structures are only a means to an end and only one way of organising one element of the council's response to perceived needs in the community;
∇   accountability for the organisation and its effectiveness must be clearly attached to people, individually or in an appropriate group.

More specifically, the management arrangements should provide for, and distinguish between:

∇   'core' operational jobs accountable for achievement of specific programmes of work;
∇   corporate support jobs, accountable for helping the council and its operational job holders plan and control their activities (to whatever degree the council or those to whom it has delegated power consent to pay for such corporate support);
∇   providers of contracted services (whether employed by the council or externally brought in) to deliver specific 'commercial' services, e.g. vehicle maintenance or catering.

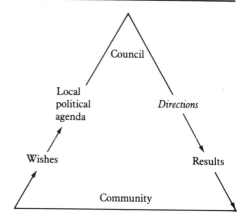

1. The organisation must be shaped to achieve the council's declared *directions* as they evolve

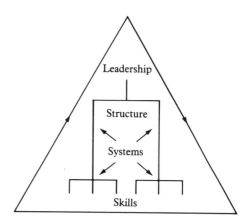

2. The structure, style and capability of the council's people and its operating processes must provide mutually complementary *management arrangements*

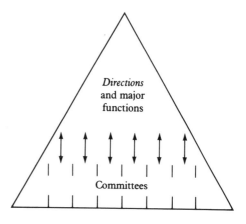

3. The core of the organisation must be shaped around the control of its *core businesses*, whether those are the provision of particular services or the achievement of more general (horizontal) *direction*

Figure 12. A set of organisational concepts

4. *Accountability* for achievement of the core businesses must be pinned on individuals who own the task of the 'whole direction' of the authority as well as the 'whole management' of priority/cost/quality in the delivery of their particular responsibility

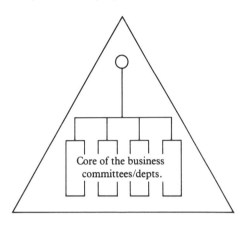

5. *Corporate supports*, agreed by the accountable directors, must provide support to the fulfilment by all directors of their accountabilities as corporate staff and as line managers

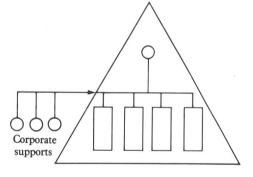

6. *Contracted services* (in-house or external) must provide specified services to quality, time, cost standards required by the accountable directors whom they serve

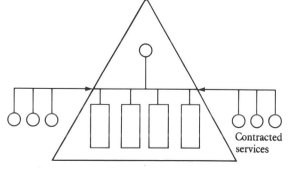

Figure 12. A set of organisational concepts (contd.)

7. *Roles and relationships in jobs*, and
contributions each to the other,
must be precisely defined, quality people appointed and developed, and their performance
reviewed

Figure 12. A set of organisational concepts (contd.)

To develop a shared framework of understanding and a set of definitions to
converse about organisational options for departments, it may be helpful to depict
what we have been saying in diagrammatic form, as in Fig. 12. Of all the points,
the last is critical. The process of definition of roles linked to the achievement of
the main purpose and *directions* of the authority will in itself amply test whether
your arrangements are appropriate to getting an authority from where it is today
to where it aims to get. We deal later with the question of people and their quality,
so we will confine ourselves for the moment to exploring in more detail the
numbered paragraphs in Fig. 12.

It will be obvious to many local authorities that education has to be regarded
as one of their main 'core' businesses. Following the principles in Fig. 12, there
will therefore be a director accountable for the provision of that service — so fundamental is it to the authority, being a major statutory obligation, committing vast
funds on services as to which local taxpayer/public/customer perceptions and
wishes are vital ingredients — and thus being a service in which the rationale for
the Widdicombe principles can be exhibited. Clearly, this is a wider accountability than 'running the Education Department'.

Whoever takes the accountability for education must necessarily be a 'main
board director' of the council's business. Some departmental heads may not be so
obviously accountable for the main business of the council and so do not qualify
for that 'core business' tag nor, therefore, a 'seat on the board'.

In the example given, 'education' is a main objective in itself for which, typically, there is a department and, perhaps, some clear *directions* from the Council
— such as 'to achieve the best skilling of the population for the existing and prospective industries of the area'. Typically, within education departments, the conventional distribution of functions into sections such as: schools (itself perhaps
divided into primary and secondary); further education; inspectorate; and so on,
do not of themselves provide an integrated answer to that sort of *direction*. Organisational options to achieve that *direction* could be various. For example, it could
be made the joint accountability of each of the third-tier officers heading up the
various functions, with a corresponding obligation upon them to liaise closely together; alternatively, one of them could be given a 'lead' accountability in some

form as a project leader; or else the deputy director might be made accountable as their line manager, or it may be decided to appoint an individual to be accountable for that specific task. If the last course is chosen, it may be that a whole organisational unit needs to be set up, together with the authority and the resources to achieve that objective. However, the notion of a 'dedicated' organisational unit is not necessarily very practicable, given that this sort of objective is one which can only be achieved through a multiplicity of contributions across the whole educational network and beyond. So while an individual can be made accountable for the achievement of the objective, the organisational support which that individual needs will not be so much through having a neat parcel of his/her own staff, but through the personal authority and credibility that the person must display — together with the consent (enforced by superior authority if necessary) of those others in the organisation whose contributions have to be blended in the achievement of that objective.

The arguments about the functional basis of a department or a section are similar to those we outlined as to whether committees should pursue vertical functional activities or horizontal tasks by subject. Such tasks will need to come and go according to changing priority objectives; once achieved, they should not become self-perpetuating 'ends' in themselves. A horizontal emphasis infers more integration and creativity in shaping and connecting different skills to make an orchestrated contribution to something which no single 'profession' can achieve. While the arguments, for and against, are similar whether we are looking at committees or departments, their roles (and those of the people involved in them) are very different. Notwithstanding the dangers of departmental tribalism, the employee 'world' needs some functional stability much more than the councillors' 'world'. In fact there is much to be said for the councillor organisation to be biased towards a continuing nomadic life across the issues of importance to the council rather than being grouped solely according to functions which, to them as members, are merely consequential.

Core businesses and corporate supports

Already it will be apparent from this brief discussion that setting up 'departments' or 'units' is neither the sole nor the most important part of the equation between objective and achievement. Rather it is the decision:

▽   who are to be in the lead and how are they to be held accountable?
▽   who are in support and at whose behest?

Let us explore these questions in relation to the distinction between the 'core of the business' departments and those which provide 'corporate support services'.

Starting from first principles, if it were not for the historic functions of education, social services, housing etc., and for the main thrusts of the *local political agenda* which elected members want to see translated into action by way of economic regeneration or the provision of leisure facilities, then there would not need to be a central finance function, personnel function, policy planning function etc. They are only there as consequences of the growth of the operational 'line' services. Moreover, if they did not exist as 'corporate' departments they would in any event have to exist in some form within the core departments. They are merely brought together corporately:

▽   to concentrate specialist expertise;
▽   to provide economies of scale;
▽   to provide for uniform standards of service, recruitment, training and career
    development in a particular profession.

They are also brought together because some of the support services are about matters of such concern to the modern local authority that they provide a critical corporate 'seam' which runs through the whole organisation, for example:

▽   the lawful exercise of statutory powers;
▽   a common financial discipline;
▽   the effective use of manpower;
▽   common information bases and research methods.

Unfortunately, this latter significance becomes distorted and the support services become dominant ends in themselves. The specialist skill of accountancy and the corporate need for a common financial discipline so dominate financial affairs that 'finance' becomes the sole property of the vertical stream represented by the Finance Committee and the Finance Department instead of a skilled service to the council's organisation. The same can be seen to be true of other well-established supports, like architecture or the secretariat's preparation of committee agendas and minutes.

So it is not only a question of such departments providing their services economically but also one of assuring their effectiveness as corporate resources for the 'staff' work we discussed in Chapter 5. Indeed, so important are some of these resources that they are as critical to the successful operation of a modern-day authority as the 'core businesses' themselves. However, the degree to which they are so recognised and are given 'seats on the board' should, as a matter of principle, be determined by the service directors accountable for the main core businesses which, at the end of the day, the support services are there to serve. To put it all at its simplest: a chief personnel officer's job should be accountable for meeting the needs of the accountable core business directors, such as housing or social services. They, in turn, should own their roles as co-directors, under the chief executive, of the whole range of the council's current concerns. This means them having a collective concern to ensure optimum professional advice, support and good practice across their departments, as well as performing their role in managing directly the work of their respective departments. After all, any corporate support services are a central overhead and only justifiable to the extent they are valued by those who employ them.

But what happens in practice?

Now contrast the propositions we have outlined with the reality of your own experience:

▽   how often do departmental directors see their role as flowing directly from,
    and to, the council through the chief executive?
▽   how often do core business departmental directors really own the job of being
    co-directors of the council's whole business?
▽   how often are corporate support departments controlled by the core busi-
    nesses as against being seen as: costly empire builders of underused services;
    or unwelcome and insensitive control agents of the chief executive or of the

typical policy sub-committees, e.g. finance, personnel, property etc.; or ineffective poseurs, accountable for nothing?

▽ how often has the treasurer dubbed it 'my' budget when it should be the core business departments' budget both as to content and the obligation to control it?

▽ how often have those same departments looked to the treasurer to provide the council with financial management information and control — notwithstanding that it should be down to them to do so?

▽ but then, how often has the council's Corporate Plan been budget-led by the traditional spending patterns of 'vertical' departments rather than by the council's current priorities balanced against overall resources?

▽ how often have we seen departments with scarcely a vestige of skills or discipline in financial or personnel management, and totally dependent upon central support departments, not so much by design but by default?

▽ how often have we seen the computer fought over as something to be owned rather than as a service to clients?

▽ how often has a central resource for the analysis of community needs and service performance been insensitively led by an elitist corporate 'centre', and/or rejected out of hand by the narrow perceptions of departments?

Contract services

We turn now to the 'contract services', by which we mean the delivery of specific services which could be obtained from outside the organisation, or are provided 'in-house' because of their likely greater efficiency, effectiveness and/or sensitivity to their users' needs. These services usually include such needs as vehicle maintenance, laundry services, catering, and cleaning, but should also be thought of in relation to the support services needed by core businesses, in addition to those provided as a corporate resource. For example, general legal advice could be made available under the corporate overhead, but specific instructions for conveyancing could be specifically charged, whether to an external or in-house solicitor.

The key question is whether the function should be provided (and therefore paid for) corporately or as part of the management of each core business. Whether, say, architecture or valuation and estate management fall into this category of a 'contract service' or into the former one of 'corporate support' depends upon the scale and importance of that function within the particular local authority. In a small district council, architecture is as likely as not best provided on a contract basis from outside — including from another district council, the county council, some other public body, or from the private sector. In a very large authority, property management may be significant enough to be a core business in itself, given the vast property holdings which are common and the better use which can be made of them to achieve the council's priorities.

Questions

▲ *1. Take the department you know best and mark it 'high', 'medium' or 'low' for its contribution under each of the 10 headings on page 75. Use your gut reactions and then test them out with other knowledgeable people.*

▲ *2. On pages 78–80 are defined seven criteria for testing the design and functioning of your organisation. How does your organisation rate on the basis of these tests?*

▲   *3. Do you think there should be more clarity of accountability between the different roles of those who:*
(a) are responsible for policy development and implementation of the 'core business' of the department/council?
(b) are responsible for providing support to them?
(c) are contracted to supply services to them?

▲   *4. Analyse the use of your time over the last year and fill in the boxes on page 73. Does the result indicate a need for different emphases?*

▲   *5. Page 74 suggests it will loosen up thinking about organisation by carrying out the hypothetical exercise of starting an organisation for the council's responsibilities from scratch. Do you know enough about the council's responsibilities to do this? If not, what information do you need and who should provide it?*

▲   *6. Try to tackle Checklist Three on pages 121–124.*

8 The organisation's people

Local authorities are all about people; their own people and the people they serve. 'Putting people first' is an incontestably appropriate philosophy to underpin the way a council manages its affairs and deserves more than lip service. It means regarding people as an investment, not a cost; being rigorous about what is needed from people; selective as to who is asked to do what; and being discriminating in reviewing their effectiveness.

Far too little care or imagination has gone into the way local authorities use their people. Moving the right people in and the wrong people out is the single most important issue: it is people who make or break the organisation. (And by 'people' we obviously must include councillors, as well as employees or the public.)

People are the critical resource

This is the shortest chapter because it needs least argument and most impact.

Little of what we have argued in this book will happen without good, motivated and skilled people. The issue of assuring quality and commitment among people — both councillors and employees — is the single most important one facing local authorities and it can only be met successfully at the top of the organisation. If the top people are right — the rest will follow.

The very essence of local authorities as 'public service orientated' businesses is sensitivity to services for people (not forgetting also what is done to people by way of taxation, regulation and the exercise of powers) through an organisation which itself is people-intensive almost like no other. People are the critical resource inside the organisation and the critical consumer force outside it. Therefore, the notion of people-sensitivity and of 'putting people first' needs to be a fundamental philosophy that should lie behind the whole of a council's thinking. Even a penny-pinching council should realise that it is people who spend the money — for good or ill! A good example of a local authority that is concerned about the potential of the people in its organisation is revealed in Fig. 13.

This is the area where we are most critical of local authorities to date, not least because they have long enjoyed the services of very skilled and dedicated people as councillors and employees. Yet their attitude to investment in people as a resource and as a *target* to influence has been lamentable. Lack of attention to the organisation's health has resulted in 'management' being too polite, too soft (both with its own staff and with councillors). It has grossly under-invested in the quality of selection, development and motivation of people and has over-invested in pure numbers. It has failed to take the huge managerial freedoms that lie there for the asking, preferring instead to be conveniently shackled by conventional practices, or the use of national negotiating systems like 'the Purple Book' as an excuse

. . . shire's strategy is to:

(a) create an open, outward-looking, problem-solving climate throughout the organisation;

(b) supplement the authority associated with role or status with the authority of knowledge and competence:

(c) locate decision-making and problem-solving responsibilities as close to the source of information as possible;

(d) build trust among individuals and groups throughout the organisation;

(e) make competition more relevant to work goals and to maximise collaborative efforts;

(f) develop reward systems which recognise both the achievement of the organisation's missions (e.g. economic provision of services) and organisation development (e.g. growth of people);

(g) increase the sense of 'ownership' of organisation objectives throughout the workforce;

(h) help managers to manage according to relevant objectives, rather than according to past practices or according to objectives which do not make sense for their area of responsibility;

(i) increase self-control and self-direction for people within the organisation;

(j) acknowledge conflict as an inherent part of organisational operations, to deal with it openly and to manage it;

(k) value increased participation in decision-making, planning and information sharing;

(l) revise our concepts of power and authority;

(m) value the development of employees as people, encouraging greater degrees of commitment, responsibility and personal awareness;

(n) place an emphasis on the need for change to keep pace with the organisation's changing strategies.

Figure 13. What sort of an organisation are we trying to create?

for avoiding purposeful local personnel policies. It has been happy to engage in labyrinthine discussion about the design of complex budgeting systems and to spend millions in computer developments. It spends untold hours considering quite small items of expenditure. Yet it has done virtually nothing by way of thoughtful planning, investment, development or hard-edged management in relation to its people. Neither has management taken much care to explore systematically the real needs and perceptions of the people in its actual marketplace, let alone 'sell' its ideas and achievements to them. (This is not the place to explore this, but the theme will be taken up in Kieron Walsh's book in this series on *Marketing*.)

The need to discriminate

The inadequacies of top management teams, both as to individual competence and collective collaboration, have been tolerated by chief executives, by team members themselves and by councillors. The same criticism can be levelled equally at councillors in respect of their own organisation. Indeed, both the 'councillor' and the 'employee' sides, through their respective committees and professional departments have allowed themselves to remain like stagnant oxbows while the main river has cut the corner and taken a different channel. Internal and external communications have been ad hoc and unplanned. Induction, training and development (especially of members) have been badly neglected. Disciplined performance planning and appraisal of individual job holders' expected contributions have been regarded as unseemly or too difficult. Happily, the tide is turning, and the challenge to engage the universally important resource of the organisation's people is being taken up by the more perceptive and determined authorities.

Alan Fowler's book, next in the series, will be pursuing many of these subjects to which we also may return another day. From them, however, we would select just one, and communicate one uncompromising message. That is about the selection for and removal of people from office.

We are unimpressed both with the quality of job definition and the recruitment process in defining the real results required of jobs (as against the activities they are asked to perform) and the relationship of one job to others. In the case of employee jobs, short-list selection, pre-interview screening and interview technique is poor. There is an absurd reluctance to use psychological assessment of personality and aptitude testing. Authorities continue to give minimal time or attention to good recruitment and totally ignore the cost to them of the money and missed opportunities represented by several years' employment of the wrong person. They also ignore the damage done to the individual who is inappropriately selected, and the frustration of the colleagues saddled with the choice.

Most serious of all, however, is their preparedness to continue allowing people to remain in post who have been over-promoted, who are inappropriate in style and manner, who are in the wrong job for their skills, or who are plainly incompetent. In all our work we have found that the question of getting the right people in and the wrong people out is the single most important issue in any organisation. It is people who make or break organisations — not usually their structures or their systems. Throughout the book we have set out ways of helping you focus on such things as job definition, role of departments, use of time etc. At the end of the book we invite you to complete a very simple checklist (p. 125) directed towards this issue. We stress that it is simple. It is you whom we ask to complete it, and you will not find it difficult. The fact is that although there is a considerable amount of academic and practical experience in the fields of personnel selection and development and of sophisticated techniques, the really key question of whether performance is satisfactory is one which, at the end of the day, inevitably rests on a collective and subjective view by the top people in the organisation (supported, of course, by as much objective information as possible). You do not need to indulge for months in research and analysis about this issue of people. You can come to a view on it very quickly. People make private judgments about other people all the time. The trouble is that 'corridor talk' is not made explicit, and judgments (rightly or wrongly held) are not tested either for their accuracy or as to what, practically, should be done about them. The first step is to create the will to address squarely the 'people problems', and the resolve to motivate at all subordinate levels. Where changes have to be made, there is need for patient consideration of each individual's circumstances so that the changes can be made constructively, but ducking the issue completely will lead to slackness throughout the organisation. We see it as an essential test of your commitment to the principles and practices we have argued for in this book that you are encouraged to take action in this most critical area — to the ultimate benefit both of the council's organisation and of the individuals concerned.

Of course, we are not suggesting a charter for the vengeful or shallow. But we do recognise that judgments about people are made daily and voiced daily — often behind closed doors, and this not only has to be recognised, but turned to proper effect. Whether the judgments are right or not depends upon many things — and a thorough system of performance appraisal will be the most helpful way of providing a basis for action. Satisfactory performance in every job — whether as a councillor or as an employee — should be constantly pursued.

Questions

▲   1. Tackle Checklist Four on pages 124–125.
▲   2. As a councillor/senior employee, would you recommend your job as a truly challenging and rewarding experience, worthwhile in every way? What are the disappointments? What could be done to make things better?

9 Measuring organisational achievements

If the council wants to know whether its *directions* and basic purposes are being fulfilled and to demonstrate this, it will be necessary to measure achievement. Although this is not easy, some measurement already takes place, and development of techniques will follow if the political need is realised. Try applying performance measurement to the jobs to which the council appoints councillors if you want to understand its potential. Jobs only exist to produce results.

Should the results achieved by the council's organisation be measured? Yes

Throughout this book we have emphasised the importance of practical results, and the clear allocation of accountability to individuals and groups for getting the results intended by the council. We have put forward the model of a local, democratic, political process which consciously and systematically sets its own agenda and uses the vast resources of powers, skills, land and money accumulated over many years to achieve that agenda. The achievement of the agenda dominates the council's organisation — how the council creates the agenda, how it intends the agenda to be implemented, how it controls implementation. So the starting point for assessing the contribution of any individual job holder, process or particular organisational structure is the clarity of the *directions*, strategies and plans determined by the council. The extent to which they will have practical operational meaning and receive commitment will heavily depend upon the quality of 'staff' support. The means by which they will be implemented by the council and, in particular, by its directly employed staff will depend upon the quality of the organisational arrangements. But the question still remains — are the *directions* being effectively fulfilled? If the council is really to be in control, it will want to know the answers to this question.

The traditional inattention to practical results achieved may well be a consequence of the council failing to give *directions* or the *directions* being unconnected to any meaningful operational programme. It may be a consequence of compartmentalised departments pursuing their own agendas, unlinked to the council's political processes. It may be a consequence of the democratic processes becoming overwhelmed by the pretence of 'running' standard services. But, assuming the council has carried out its responsibilities for creating an operationally meaningful *local political agenda* and has delegated responsibility for implementation to an effective arrangement of committees, departments and external agencies, the quality of its performance must be systematically assessed if the value of the existing *directions* is to be assessed and the responsibility of those in charge is to be held to account. It will not only enable decision-makers to control those who act on their behalf but will also fulfil the council's own accountability to the local community.

It is often said that the measurement of performance is difficult, if not impossible, in the public services, where there is no 'bottom line' or 'profit motive'. Employees and councillors alike are rightly wary lest quantified assessments override the importance of properly subjective judgments or encourage minor but very visible problems to distort assessment of performance in essential yet lower profile requirements. These fears are more an adverse reflection on the quality of the existing organisation and its capacity to produce information in the right context than on the potential contribution of performance measurement to better local government.

Assuming that a council's organisation is dominated by its purposes in the way we have described, how can one go about the task of measurement? The precise answer to that question will vary, because the techniques employed will depend on the reasons why, and at what level in the organisation, the council wishes to measure performance. But first let us try to establish in broad terms what we mean by 'performance' and its measurement by looking at five ways in which it is already practised in local authorities:

▽   justifying new expenditure;
▽   performance review to check 'value for money';
▽   performance management systems;
▽   government inspection;
▽   consumer assessment.

Justifying new expenditure

It is invariably a dominant feature of local authority processes that proposed new expenditure has to be justified. Control of already authorised expenditure by the political processes may be little more than nominal — e.g. the annual approval of the existing base budget — but new expenditure has to run a gauntlet of criticism as it competes in priority for scarce resources. The simple point is that the supporters of proposed expenditure will invariably try to justify its value in terms of prospective performance, and the council rarely has difficulty in reaching a judgment about whether or not the promised benefits are what it wants, or how they compare in priority with other new proposals. It is only when the expenditure has been authorised that people become coy about what it is actually achieving! 'Performance' is already measured in advance.

Performance review to check 'value for money'

Secondly, the concern to maximise 'value for money', which has been an increasingly important force in the work of local authorities, has led to the use of 'performance review' committees and increased emphasis on the work of 'management services', of internal management audit and external review by the district auditor or equivalent, and of management consultants. The quality and effectiveness of all this work varies considerably, is frequently undertaken on a fairly random basis and rarely evaluates the performance of those people at the top involved in commissioning the review. Yet when judgments about performance are about to be made, a variety of relevant and helpful information can be obtained on which judgments are reached. In November 1986, the Audit Commission published a useful handbook for auditors and local authorities on *Performance Review in Local Government* to help people answer the questions:

▽   are we providing value to the public we serve?
▽   how do we know this — and can we show it?
▽   what are the key issues facing us and what are we doing to address them?

The continued development of this work promised by the Commission will provide an expanding technical basis for coping with the 'how?'

Performance management systems

A third use of performance measurement in recent years has been in evaluating the contribution of individual employees on a systematic basis. Ideally, the system will begin with job design linked to the council's objectives, followed by setting performance plans and targets, evaluating achievement, and providing training, career development and rewards as a consequence. If an individual's achievement of set targets can be measured, then aggregate achievements of aggregate targets by a section, by a department, or by the whole council can be measured also, drawing upon good existing information and stimulating its improvement.

Government inspection

A fourth use of performance measurement, with which local authorities have long been familiar, is the renewal of specific grant, dependent upon performance to the satisfaction of Whitehall. The judgment of HM Inspectors of Constabulary, for example, about the efficiency of the local police force is based on annual review of the professional peformance of the chief constable, and the different sections of the force. Other specific grants, e.g. Transport Supplementary Grant, are more tied to proposed expenditure than past performance, but it should not be difficult to create performance measures from the justifying claims and cost/benefit analyses made for the grant in the first place.

Consumer assessment

A fifth approach, which is gaining acceptance, is that of consumer assessment. A good way of finding out whether the services which the council provides are meeting the needs which persuaded it to allocate resources is to ask the recipients. The National Consumer Council's report *Measuring Up* (1986) attempts 'to provide some way of finding what services do for consumers and whether they effectively achieve their objectives'. The report is a valuable addition to the accumulating body of technical knowledge, and complements the Local Government Training Board's strong promotion of service for and with the public rather than to the public,[9] and its summary of ten principles applicable to good practice (p. vii) is particularly helpful.

It is therefore apparent that performance is already being measured in a variety of ways and that a useful grounding in techniques is already available for practitioners. The challenge is to apply and develop them so that they serve the purposes of

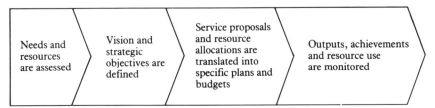

Source: Introduction to Performance Review in Local Government. A Handbook for Auditors and local authorities. Audit Commission. HMSO 1986, p.6.

Figure 14. Performance measurement

the council as part of its iterative processes for shaping *direction*, strategy and plans, controlling implementation and then reshaping *direction*, strategy and plans in the light of practical results, the whole being simply expressed as in Fig. 14.

Performance measurement should be related to the needs of each level of authority and to the fulfilment of all its fundamental purposes

When performance measurement forms part of the kind of iterative process just described rather than as an ad hoc result of one of the five approaches just described — or any other approach — it is obvious that the kind of measurement undertaken will have to relate to the accountability of the particular person or group whose performance is being measured. The broad impacts which it may be appropriate to examine when considering the council's achievements will usually be inappropriate when considering the performance of a middle manager, and vice versa. As one moves down through the levels of authority of the council, committee/sub-committee, chief officer, senior manager etc., the precision of measurement will increase because the accountabilities discharged are that much more focused on specifics. Delegation can only be granted with confidence if the performance of delegates can be assessed and their accountability enforced. Freedom given to committees and to individuals to take initiatives on behalf of the council should be accompanied by an accountability for results achieved, so the creation of processes for enforcing accountability may be necessary before the extensive and firmly enforced delegation advocated in Chapter 4 is acceptable to the council. Even so, there is always some delegation: whatever it is should provoke a corresponding accountability for results.

Running through all the levels of authority will be the practical *directions* articulated by the council in meeting its fundamental purposes — the purposes of political pluralism, democratic participation and sensitive local service delivery identified by Widdicombe. The processes of measurement will have to account for all three attributes if the whole of the council's purposes are to be dealt with. The emphasis should not be on service delivery alone. It is interesting to see how these fundamental purposes are applied to performance measurement in the three publications just mentioned. The Audit Commission handbook (Introduction, pp. 3–4) emphasises local authority accountability to the public for the services provided, and better management of expenditure at a time of changing social and economic circumstances:

Performance review can enhance accountability by:

1. demonstrating success in achieving policy aims efficiently, economically and effectively;
2. highlighting aspects of services where further enquiry and explanation is needed;
3. making the responsibilities and achievements of staff explicit.

Performance review can assist in the change towards active management by:

1. providing a basis for policy planning and control;
2. enabling activities to be monitored at various levels in relation to council policies;
3. providing information for the review of policies, management practices and methods.

The main emphasis is on the sensitivity of service delivery, with a subsidiary acknowledgment of democratic participation.

The National Consumer Council report, written from a different point of view, stresses the need for facts, rather than abstract political argument, in helping the consumer to evaluate whether value for money is being provided, and shifts the emphasis of the value for money debate from 'money' to 'value'. The authors of the report set themselves two objectives: 'to encourage local authorities to set explicit targets for their "consumer performance" and to evaluate and report on their achievement, and to provide local government consumers with information which will enable them to raise questions about the performance of their authorities' (p. ii). Again the emphasis is mainly on sensitive service delivery.

The Local Government Training Board paper by Michael Clark and John Stewart titled *Getting Closer to the Public* starts with the following five principles:

▽ a local authority's activities exist to provide service for the public;
▽ a local authority will be judged by the quality of service provided within the resources available;
▽ the service provided is only of real value if it is of value to those for whom it is provided;
▽ those for whom services are provided are customers demanding high-quality service;
▽ quality of service demands closeness to the customer.

The priority of service delivery is again clear but perhaps inevitable, given the focus of the paper on service provision.

Although performance measurement appropriate to a local authority is therefore still at an early stage of development, from this emerging corpus of thought and practice can be developed systems of data collection, validation and presentation tailor-made to suit the requirements of each council and each level of decision-making in their organisation. The overall emphasis will depend upon each council's understanding of its fundamental business purposes, its consequential political choices and its practical strategies for achievement. The emphasis at each level will depend upon the terms of delegation. Ideally, one is aiming for a set of inter-related processes of performance planning and measurement in which the eventual achievements in the job of each individual councillor or employee build up to the results which, collated and generalised through various groupings, constitute the overall achievements sought by the council.

Apply performance measurement to the jobs of councillors for insight into its potential influence

It is not only the employees who contribute to the council's achievements or failures. Councillors individually and collectively also contribute under all three basic purposes. The statement is so obvious that councillors will be affronted that it is thought worthwhile to make it. Yet in how many councils is there serious evaluation of the success of the council as a local political institution? In how many councils are the specialist jobs like committee chairman, party whip, leader of the opposition, or committee member, specifically written down as job descriptions on which to base assessment of performance, let alone as a basis for their selection and skills development?

At a time when the local authority model of local government is under threat, what demonstrable facts are available to justify its democratic value locally? If sensitive local services delivery is the only aspect of a local authority's basic purpose which is evaluated, for how much longer can the values of political pluralism and democratic participation be taken for granted? Service delivery is more visible and conventionally capable of measurement. Evaluation of the latter two purposes is more judgmental and 'closer to the bone' politically. But if the council is not robust enough to see them as essential elements of its fabric which equally require evaluation, it is lending its silence to opponents of local democracy and failing to highlight its contribution to self-government. The responsibility of a councillor to the electorate for performance as a councillor may not be an appropriate subject for evaluation by any other process than re-election, but evaluation of achievement in the jobs the council creates for councillors, although they are largely unpaid, is essential if the political achievements of the council are to be communicated and judged.

The suggestion that a councillor's performance can and should be evaluated as part of the council's assessment of its collective performance arises naturally from consideration of the purpose of performance measurement — yet the idea will come as a shock to many people. Consideration of the suggestion underlines six important points of general application:

▽   that determined and realistic performance measurement must be sensitive to the particular situation of those being appraised, and command their respect by their substantial involvement in the advance selection of appropriate measures and the design of the measurement processes. Few councillors would consent to their performance being appraised on any other terms!

▽   that once the process of performance measurement is begun, it leads on to exploration of the contribution of people hitherto thought of as beyond question;

▽   that the political answers to the question 'Why do we want performance measurement?' and the follow-through of their implications by councillors, and for councillors, will be far more important in impact on the design of the performance measurement processes than the currently perceived limits of available official techniques;

▽   that the consequences of noting achievements or failures should be sufficiently serious to make the effort of measurement worthwhile;

▽   that any one measure of a person's or a group's performance is likely to be unfair if taken in isolation;

▽   that although some achievements are the sole responsibility of each individual, the quality of corporate achievements by the council relies heavily on
contributions from people working together to create synergy.

Let us take these points one by one.

Participation

While officers may be able to assist in designing forms of words or processes,
only the councillors can know what it is to be a councillor, or can authorise a view
about the expected results of good committee chairmanship, or can be realistic
about the extent of agreement across the political spectrum on the value of the
democratic process and ways of accounting to the electorate. In just the same way,
only those actually familiar with classroom teaching in a particular school can
realistically say what achievements can be expected in the education of a particular
class. Fortunately it is found by experience that people rarely overrate their own
potential achievement and, of course, the line management system should be
designed to ensure realistic standards of achievement.

Ever-extending appraisal

A colleague consultant from overseas recently told us of a timber company
client concerned to improve productivity. The loggers in the forest were involved
in setting weekly targets relating to safety, delivery, waste etc. and made considerable efforts to achieve them, spurred by various incentives. When, on the Monday
following, the first recorded total achievements were not available, there was great
disappointment. When the next Monday was equally disappointing the loggers
began to question the contribution of the supervisory and clerical staff responsible. The inadequacy of explanations about other priority work, when the company had obviously made increased productivity of timber its first priority, was
obvious. The 'central overheads' of the company, hitherto unquestioned, were
soon made the subject of performance measurement from the workforce! The
same consultant takes his own medicine. His own share of profits depends partly
on assessments of his contribution by his support staff. His timeliness in giving
material to the typist, his regularity in keeping in touch with the office, his general
thoughtfulness for the work of colleagues, all contribute to the effectiveness of the
consultancy. Why shouldn't he be subject to such formal assessment? Why
shouldn't you, councillor? You are frequently assessed informally!

Dominated by purpose not techniques

The assertion of clear, political purpose, supported and implemented by
technical skills, is the recurrent theme of this book. It applies to performance
measurement too. The danger of waiting for an approved technical model of
appraisal to be devised is that it will not carry political conviction and will just become a fashionable routine — like the traditional annual budget process. As we
have said, information that is relevant to elected member concerns is rarely going
to be the same as that which is relevant for assessment of an individual employee.
Indeed, if the information relating to the assessment of each employee were to be
put before the council, it would be cumulatively overwhelming in all but the very
smallest councils — though the capacity of many councils for accepting an un-

reasonable volume of agenda material has to be acknowledged! If the council were able to express its *directions* for controlling the work of the authority in terms of targeted measurable achievements, the linking of this information to the resources allocated for the purpose to committees and by committees to departments and sections would begin to make sense even of the traditional annual budget!

Importance of consequences

For the loggers, in the example just given, their pride in achieving targets and the recognition of their efforts by the employer were at stake. For the consultant, it was part of his bonus. For the asphalting gang in the direct labour organisation, their bonus and the estimated costs in future competitive tenders will be at stake. For councillors, the achievement of a higher profile for local political issues through their handling of meetings and public relations should give considerable satisfaction in their concern to justify the value of the local political processes and might well influence the selection and continued existence of councillors in the future. Since the successful measurement of achievement depends very considerably on the realistic setting of achievement targets, few people will give priority to the time and energy involved unless the consequences are sufficiently important.

Inter-relationship of measures

The performance of some very straightforward tasks can easily be measured by a single clear statistic. The productivity of a machine may be judged by the number of widgets produced per minute. But few human jobs have only one important feature. Speed may have to be balanced by the need for accuracy, for safety, for courtesy and many other important considerations. Nor can quality usually be judged in a hard, statistical way, though some judgment can be made, for example, about the number of complaints. But even the number of complaints requires careful examination. How many of the complaints are 'reasonable'? Immediately we are into a world of subjective judgments. But subjective judgments are made anyway. The difference between a system of formal annual appraisal of a subordinate's performance by the line manager and the absence of such a system will rarely lie in the presence or absence of subjective judgments. In the former case, an adverse judgment will be expressed, can be challenged, and methods of improvement discussed. In the latter case, embarrassed non-communication, mutual frustration and poor results will often be tolerated until a destructive crisis has to be coped with. The basis of successful measurement will invariably relate to the kind of judgments which are informally made, irrespective of the existence of a formal system. The formal system enables the subjective and the objective judgments to be seen together, to be discussed by reviewer and reviewed, and to be linked to appropriate action.

Mutual dependency

The allocation of clear accountabilities under the council's scheme of delegation has been discussed in the last chapter. But the realistic view of other people's linked contributions which has to be made when setting achievement targets for an individual or a group will help to clarify and improve the often confused relationships between, say, the authority and Whitehall, or between different groups within the council's organisation, over who is accountable for what, and where the accountability has to be shared. The jobs to which the council appoints councillors obviously cannot be fulfilled in isolation from the rest of the organisation, or from other organisations.

The successful introduction of performance measurement requires political commitment to the importance of the *targets* to be achieved and to appropriate action when they are not achieved. Revision to less ambitious *targets* or improvement of funding is at one end of the scale of possibilities (but within the discipline of the council's *directions*), and removal of people (councillors and/or employees) from the jobs in which they have failed at the other. It requires high-quality 'staff' support to systematise and process the measures, and a competent, well-defined line of management to ensure realistic targets and their purposeful achievement. Performance measurement need not be related to pay, but achievements which have been hard won should certainly produce reward in terms of recognition, career advancement, training opportunities and greater freedom to take initiatives. Performance measurement is a challenging discipline because it directly asks the question 'Have you made the contribution reasonably expected of you towards the results determined by the council?' Jobs, whether elected or appointed, exist to produce results. They are not there just as seats to be sat on.

Questions

▲   *1. Do you have clear, comparative, regular evidence of whether your council is making a real impact in relation to the issue you identified when dealing with Question 1 of Chapter 1 on page 14?*

▲   *2. Taking the five methods of performance measurement referred to on pages 90–92, which of them might be developed to challenge and justify the existence of the parts of the organisation for which you have a responsibility — especially in relation to the issue you identified when dealing with Question 1 of Chapter 1 on page 14?*

▲   *3. How can the council demonstrate the value of its locally elected governors? How can it show the result it has achieved from its use of its resources and its influence? It may be helpful just to limit your consideration to the issue you identified when dealing with Question 1 of Chapter 1 on page 14.*

E

10 Organising the councillors' jobs

In addition to their democratic, representative job, in which they are all equal, councillors have a variety of jobs to do, and bring a variety of skills and potential contributions. They need to ask themselves whether the job of being a councillor in their council as set up, and supported, to be satisfying and worthwhile, or whether they follow a conventional stereotype of interminable meetings about detail, rather than direction, and the processing of other people's agendas rather than their own. If they define their jobs and review their performance, that will show up the ways they can be helped to improve their contributions.

Stick to what matters most

Throughout the book we have argued that councillors (not just officers) have jobs to do, that there are different ways of organising for the job in hand, different roles to be distinguished and exercised, and different skills to be employed. At the same time, these all have to be integrated so that the local authority works coherently. This requires sensitive handling at the top through the chief executive, his colleague co-directors and leading councillors. It also requires discipline to prevent the issues that are more appropriately handled through one particular process not being allowed to stray into others. For example, if operational management is to be truly delegated to accountable officers, then it must not be sucked back into routine committee supervision by councillors (major sensitive items excepted, of course). But this will tend to happen if councillors do not focus their attention on giving their employees clear *directions*. Delegation cannot work if it is not clear to the delegates what they are there to achieve. Councillors must carve out the time for themselves to give those *directions*. Senior employees must help them to do this and pay as much regard to their accountability, as 'support staff' to the council, as they do to leading their own professional departments.

The stereotype structure of many local authorities, with a fairly large number of service-based committees plus a corresponding department and chief officer, results in the latter creating most of the agenda. The principle of 'if in doubt, leave it in' and the curse of the photocopying machine means that councillors are hard put to read the quantity of paper that lands on their doorsteps, let alone find the time to have minds of their own! They constantly complain of not having the framework and information to discuss the things they want to discuss rather than having to cope with a heavy menu of someone else's choosing. It is as much (in fact more of) an obligation for the support staff to correct this imbalance as it is for the councillors to demand it to be done. After all, this expertise is what the support staff are paid for!

The distribution of councillors' time in any given local authority can be checked against the following two pictures of the way time may be spent. How much does it feel like the first, or the second . . .?

If . . .

▽   'information' items are circulated separately or in different ways;
▽   less time is spent on the approval of protocol and administrative issues;
▽   more accountability is placed on staff both to deliver against clearly articulated *directions*, and against managerial performance standards;
▽   exploratory discussions are carefully and separately processed.

Then . . .

▽   the more time and care can be taken in determining *directions* and strategies with achievable and properly resourced plans;
▽   and more open, enquiring, relevant and rewarding exploration of local needs, ideas and initiatives can take place.

A council needs to apply the acid test of 'performance review' to its effectiveness in carrying out its own role. If it is unable to say that it is fully satisfied that it systematically focuses on the setting of *directions* and review of peformance, then it is not managing itself, and attention should be given to the ideas in this chapter and in Chapter 1 about 'the business of a local council' (p. 8).

Thus far we have argued:

▽   that it is a critical, continuing priority for a local authority to be concerned with its organisational health (Chapter 1);
▽   that in exercising its roles to govern, to pursue a local political agenda and to manage its operations, there are differing ways and means of achieving those tasks (Chapters 6 and 7).

We now go on to argue:

▽   that as the above imply different roles and different ways of managing them, it will also be obvious that a variety of different commitments, contributions and skills are needed from (and brought by) councillors, and that a number of distinct jobs have to be done by them.

Using councillors' skills

Quite apart from their differing leanings as individuals, their political persuasions, special concerns about the locality and so forth, councillors also come with a range of backgrounds and skills which may include, for example:

▽   specific professional skills;
▽   promotional and communicational skills;
▽   political seasoning and shrewdness;
▽   diplomacy;
▽   ability to conduct meetings;
▽   maturity and common sense;
▽   barometer of community interests;
▽   membership of other public authorities;
▽   financial discipline;
▽   business planning;

▽   entrepreneurial flair;
▽   staff relations;
▽   management of other complex organisations.

The challenge is to attract and to engage these skills by raising the level of practical, local, political challenges to be faced and encouraging councillors to face them. Most councils do have some means of discovering from councillors what their special interests are and of fitting them to the committees they prefer to be on. But this is basically just a way of allocating people to 'seats'. The standing assumption is that being a councillor means 'sitting on committees'. At least it is predictable, and the other councillors and senior employees know where they are and what they are up to — at least for the time they are behind the committee-room doors!

In practice, of course, while skills do gravitate to posts, the selection process is not very explicit. These days, with higher turnover of councillors (many of whose terms of office do not last more than the life of a council), the time during which their skills can be quickly focused is more and more limited. The frustrations at not being able to contribute one's best may also be a reason for not standing for election again. Serving one's apprenticeship through the 'minor' committees was a laborious process in the authorities of the past, and though less exaggerated today, it is still there.

The democratic environment also inevitably works against a differential distribution of jobs and in favour of 'fair shares of committee seats for all'. 'All councillors are equal.' After all, this is not a business organisation where one expects to find different functions, different sizes of jobs, different roles and different sorts of contributions — like those in 'the line' and those 'in support'. Or is it? Of course it is!

We would argue two points. First, that councillors' skills and interests need to be engaged more quickly and productively to enable them to make their best possible contribution. This applies to all of them. Second, that councillors do actually have jobs in their organisations, in addition to their democratic role as representative in which indeed they are all equals.

Members' jobs

The job of mayor is different to that of leader, which in turn is different from the job of committee chairman, and so on. This may appear obvious in practice, but how often are these jobs made explicit so that everyone is clear about the role, and hence its selection and performance requirements? If employees' jobs are expected to be clear and accountable for good performance, why not the jobs of councillors? Each needs the other to be effective. After all, in the outside world there are different levels of contribution within an organisation, as shown in Fig. 15.

But there are vertical 'levels' of contribution, based on structure and authority. There are other contributions which need to run across the concerns of the council, or in phases — and which are not about authority, but about creating different links in a chain of events. They imply different skills — and also a passing of the baton — thus team working (Fig. 16).

In a local authority committee there could well be a need, not just for the conventional role of a chairman but for roles such as 'promoters' and 'implementers'.

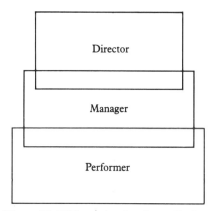

Figure 15. Different levels of contribution

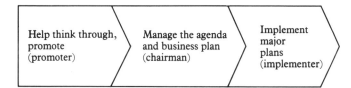

Figure 16. Lateral contributions

This is not to say we suggest a whole hierarchy of jobs for councillors but simply to point to the fact that it is possible, indeed vital, to engage the contributions of different councillors, find satisfying roles for them and ensure that everything is not 'down to' the chairman.

Most chairmen will be better at some things than others. There is no reason to expect of a chairman (or for a chairman to attempt) the exercise of several roles at once. Suffice it that he/she is at least able to bridge the worlds of the elected member and the employed agents of the council and to organise a planned programme of work for the committee during the year, help to ensure that the presentation of its business is thorough and economical, that councillors' skills are drawn in and developed and that productive discussion and decisions come out of the process. If he/she is also a leader of major initiatives, an external promoter, and enjoys a good relationship with the employees, then so much the better. However, if he/she is a good manger of the committee's business (and secures the consent of colleagues to that role), then it is more important for the chairman to be thinking about how to engage other councillors in this task and keep some control of thinking space in order to have time for working out how affairs should best be handled, whether how to drive through a major initiative or to respond to a crisis.

Of course, the more the council (and its senior employees) begin to look for different ways to supplement its formal committee processes — such as exploratory seminars and working groups — the more opportunities there will be for councillors' skills and interest to emerge. But it also has to be said that there are risks. Are the people concerned really capable of making the leap of faith which allows them to free their thinking and attitudes away from the comfortable predictability of operating through 'set piece' committees where councillors and employees each 'know their place'? It would be naive to pretend that every council can or even should do this in the short term. It may well be very important for a council to hang on to the conventional disciplines of committee-run business during times of major political strife among its members! Even where there is a strong majority and stability, the idea of opening up discussion through seminars, and of seeking all-party involvement in working groups may be treated (often very justifiably) with the suspicion that councillors will not play to the rules, but to the gallery. Councillors need to try and hold back from taking cheap advantage of privileged information and open-ended thinking in the cause of improving the quality of their overall responsiveness and judgment as to local needs and their mission to 'govern'.

If that is the spirit we want to keep alive, then councillors must exercise self-discipline, which has to be voluntary: it is not susceptible to formal regulation. Local government, if it is to be effective, must be managed, just as a local authority's services must be managed. So we turn to our earlier assertion that there are distinct jobs to be undertaken within the 'elected organisation'. If the council's business is to be managed, then there must be managers of it from their (the councillors') side with some clarity and acknowledgment of the sort of roles that need to be played. Most councils define in their formal delegations to committees some clear parcelling out of powers and duties. It is only a short step from there to write down the roles of various councillors who are appointed to carry them out. Let us look at two of them in detail: the role of a typical committee chairman (or of a small group of members in a 'hung' council) and the role of the chairman of the council, or mayor.

Two examples: 'chairing' a committee, and 'chairing' the council

In each case we start with a short statement of overall purpose and then set out a list of 'principal accountabilities'. These are drafted so as to focus on the result which is required. Whether or not the reader agrees with the precise wording is by the way. The purpose of setting out these accountabilities is to focus attention on the main aspects of the job that need to be addressed. In the columns on the right of the page there is the means of checking how well the role is exercised at the moment and what sort of priority the incumbent might decide to attach to each accountability during the coming year. In the first column you can 'score' current performance with a number, choosing between 5 (outstanding), 4 (superior), 3 (fully acceptable), 2 (marginal), 1 (poor). In the second column, indicate the priority for attention in the next 12 months: H (high), M (medium), L (low).

Possible job profile for chairman of committee

PRINCIPAL ACCOUNTABILITIES	Current Performance 5–1	Priority for Attention H M L
1. *Policy determination and review* Enable the committee to determine strategies within overall council *directions* and to integrate them with the objectives and programmes of other services, in order to assure their relevance to changing local		

	Current Performance 5–1	Priority for Attention H M L

needs and statutory obligations — based on systematic review of the effectiveness with which they meet their declared aims.

2. *Operational planning and control*
    Ensure that plans and budgets are proposed, implemented and controlled which enable the achievement of the committee's approved strategies within cash limits.

3. *Organisational effectiveness*
    Ensure that the service's internal organisation is adequate for the fulfilment of the council's aims, is efficiently operated and staffed by competent, motivated people, and supported by the relevant councillors.

4. *Councillor roles*
    Ensure that the exercise of councillor roles in relation to the committee is undertaken with adequate information and advice, conforms with proper procedures and that members have adequate induction and continuing training to be able to contribute effectively.

5. *Councillor and councillor/officer relationships*
    Develop good communications and relationships between the councillors (both within the committee and council-wide) and with chief officers and other senior employees to secure mutual understanding and collaboration.

6. *Internal/external collaboration*
    Secure purposeful joint planning and working with other council services through their accountable chairmen, and with other relevant bodies and authorities, in order to exploit fully the opportunities for economic and effective use of their total potential resources.

7. *Public relations*
    Promote public awareness of the council's and the committee's objectives, constraints and achievements so as to generate the greatest possible understanding and good relations with the public.

Readers may well now be asking 'Doesn't that sound like the job of the chief officer?' Indeed it does, but the difference is that the chairman and committee are there to ensure that these things are done, not to do them themselves. If they accept accountability for that, and there are no costs for examining and improving their performance, then why are they there?

Next follows a definition of the job of the chairman of the council. This assumes the classic role as chairman of the full meeting of the council and that the role is expected to be operated in an apolitical way, such political groups as there are having separate leaders. It also assumes a statesman-like role, concerned with the health and integrity of the council's affairs and its external image.

Possible job profile for chairman of council/mayor

JOB PURPOSE

To steer the council towards constructive debate wherein different interests are democratically balanced and the establishment of clear forward directions for the organisation to take action; .
to ensure that the constitution is observed; to develop and govern the effective and proper conduct and organisation of councillors and their relations with employees;
to ensure the development and support of councillors in performing their roles most effectively;
to promote the purposes and reputation of the council.

PRINCIPAL ACCOUNTABILITIES

	Current Performance 5–1	Priority for Attention H M L

1. *Council meetings*
Ensure that the business of the council is con-ducted efficiently and constitutionally, that the forum is used for the constructive debate and resolution of clear strategic directions which maximise member agreement and commitment in the interests of the authority as a whole while permitting the ventilation of different views without loss of momentum of estab-lished policy or the reputation of the authority.

2. *Distribution of council functions among councillors*
In conjunction with the chief executive and party leaders, keep under review the distribution of func-tions between, and organisation of, councillors in the conduct of the council's affairs so that the planning and delivery of services and the representation of particular interests fulfils the council's democratic purposes.

3. *Councillors' information and support services*
Ensure that councillors have the information and administrative support to enable them to exercise their roles effectively.

4. *Councillors' jobs and training*
Ensure that the jobs entailed in being a councillor are clearly known to prospective candidates, and in-

cumbents, and that induction and continuing training and development is undertaken so that councillors may be attracted who are capable of performing these jobs.

Current Performance 5–1   *Priority for Attention H M L*

5. *Councillors' skills and interests*

Develop and monitor the ways in which all councillors are enabled to contribute their particular skills and interests in ways appropriate to the representation of their electorate and their collective task of meeting authority-wide needs.

6. *Councillor and officer obligations and relationships*

Ensure that the obligations, rights and respect which councillors and employees both have for and owe to the council and to each other are upheld, so that they conduct themselves appropriately and in a collaborative climate for joint working.

7. *Public relations*

Promote good relations with local authorities, and other public bodies, the press and the electorate so that effective working relationships are maintained between them and that the reputation of the authority is upheld.

8. *Promotion and representation of the council*

Represent the council on official occasions, host its guest and promote its purposes and achievements so that these may be respected and supported.

9. *Propriety*

Ensure that standards of propriety are laid down, promulgated and enforced.

What about the 'backbencher'?

Finally, let us attempt a job profile for the basic role of a councillor. As in the other two examples, the role is seen not just as a platform for what a councillor wants to do but carries obligations to contribute more widely (as argued before, making best use of his/her skills and interests) and also be concerned to support the health and reputation of the council as an effectie means of local government. Otherwise there won't be any local government to be elected to! While councillors have the right to exercise their role by virtue of their election to the office, the only way the council will be effective as a whole is through engaging their collaborative commitment to its fundamental purposes even though on many important issues they will disagree with each other.

Possible job profile for an elected member

JOB PURPOSE

To represent the condition and wishes of their division/ward and to secure a collaborative relationship between the public, the council and other related bodies; contribute to the formulation and review of council *directions* for the provision of council services in meeting local needs and for their funding and control.

PRINCIPAL ACCOUNTABILITIES	*Current Performance*	*Priority for Attention*
1. *Constituency needs*	*5–1*	*H M L*

Inform the council's organisation of conditions and concerns within the constituency so as to enable a balanced appreciation to be gained of the problems and opportunities which are open to the council's influence.

2. *Authority-wide policies*
   Contribute to the formulation and review of *directions* for the provision of services which are appropriate and affordable in meeting local needs across the area consistently and within the statutory obligations of the authority.

3. *Resource allocation*
   Contribute to the determination of how resources should be acquired and allocated so that adequate funds are available and purposefully applied, to the implementation of approved council *directions*.

4. *Effectiveness review*
   Participate as required in the formal review of both policy and service operations to assist the council in satisfying itself as to their continued effectiveness in meeting approved objectives.

5. *Appointments*
   Perform the duties of such internal or external jobs to which he/she may be appointed so as to contribute effectively to the conduct of the council's business and the advancement of its interests.

6. *Internal/external collaboration*
   Secure purposeful collaboration with other elected councillors, employees, local and special interest groups in order to realise the best application of skills and resources in meeting local needs.

7. *Public relations*
   Promote local awareness of the council's policies and programmes, its achievements and constraints so as to generate the greatest possible understanding by and good relations with the public.

8. *Personal development*
   Keep abreast of developments and practices in the council's organisation and in local government generally, and undertake personal training in order to be

continually better able to contribute to the conduct of
council affairs, internally and externally.

Each election offers the opportunity of communicating the expected standards of content and conduct of councillors' roles — just in the same way as when
an employee is appointed. People need to know what is expected of them, both in
achieving the results for which they are accountable and in helping others
associated with them to achieve theirs. Given that there are different roles to be
performed, it is not unreasonable to define what they should be. It is even possible
to tread into sensitive areas such as the definition of key elements of the jobs of
leaders of the various groups. For example, one of their accountabilities could be
worked out as follows:

> as leader of the council, work with the chairman of the council, the lead-
> ers of the other parties/groups and the chief executive, to ensure that the
> maximum common ground is agreed upon. Where significant differing
> views are held enable these to be positively debated without detriment to
> the forward momentum of established policy or the public reputation of
> the council.

If it is accepted that there are different sorts of jobs to be carried out among
councillors and different sorts of contribution to be made by them, then both
councillors and their senior advisers need to be thoughtful about how this is to be
recognised in practice and provided for:

▽   in the support that is given to those jobs to enable them to be performed effec-
     tively;
▽   in the preparation and choice of candidates for the various jobs (including
     prospective councillors in the first place);
▽   by selecting what time is spent on what priorities;
▽   in appraising and developing effectiveness in the various jobs;
▽   in establishing effective working relationships.

Play fair, and avoid 'own goals'

The council needs to decide policies, vote resources, implement efficiently and review effectiveness. It should be common ground among all parties that the *process*
of doing this should be acceptable and efficient. Similarly, once a particular policy
has been decided, maximising the benefits from its implementation should be the
concern of all. Even if a particular group of them disagree with a traffic scheme,
they should be concerned to see that it is well implemented, and then can pursue
their opposition in the light of its performance. After all, good management will
be what they will look for when it comes to 'their schemes' being implemented,
and poor management reduces the stock of the council as an effective means of
local government.

If it is accepted that councillors should strive to find and build upon the common ground they have, as well as generating robust argument and creative tension, then they will the more easily be able to make a constructive rather than a
destructive contribution at various stages in the process of defining and achieving
the council's *local political agenda*.

| | | 'Ends' | | |
| | | 'Ways and means' | | |
The council needs to ...	Decide policy →	Agree means & resources →	Implement efficiently →	Review effectiveness
The majority	Determine	Direct	Support	Scrutinise
The opposition	Challenge	Test	Examine	Scrutinise
The hung parties	Share	Consent to	Support	Scrutinise
The officers	Recommend	Develop	Execute	Scrutinise

Figure 17. Differentiated contributions

Figure 17 assumes some fairly standard reactions within a council to the processes of debate about 'policy' options. Alter the words you would use for your own council, if there are significant differences.

The paradox is that in many councils there is more discussion and argument about the two middle columns than there is about the two each side of them. The 'ends' become lost in the argument about expenditure and about operational efficiency — the 'ways and means'. Surely the local electorate, as well as the organisation, is entitled to have a clearer picture of the competing policy choices and the effectiveness of the chosen ones. If a council, as the decisive voice of democratic local government, is to live up to that purpose, the ballot paper should not just reflect some national political swing or perceptions about the efficiency of the current administration, but should be an expression of support for certain policy choices and their proven effectiveness. Majority parties who hang on to power without clear, local, operationally meaningful policies or any rigorous assessment of their effects are neither governing nor furthering the cause of 'local government'. Similarly, opposition parties who are merely destructive and proffer no clear, local, operationally meaningful alternatives are equally useless. The survival of local government requires more of councillors than to immerse themselves in operational detail and irrelevant argument. Their job is to determine a *local political agenda*, give clear directions to their officers, ensure that there is an effective, healthy organisation to deliver results and a rigorous review of that organisation's continued effectiveness — undismayed and constructive when policy weaknesses are revealed and, needless to say, pleased when they aren't.

The kind of politicisation which local authorities now need to embrace should not be about pale imitations of the national political divisions but about the defence of the purposes of local government and the promotion of solutions which will meet local needs. The many parts that councillors play in their council should at least all be played in such a way as to meet these overriding objectives.

Questions

▲   *1. Do your committee agendas and forms of meetings enable councillors to think through, decide and review the things that matter most to them in discharging their responsibilities as councillors? What changes would you like to see? Do other people agree with you? If it helps, use the issue you identified when dealing with Question 1 of Chapter 1 on page 14 as an example.*

▲   *2. What are the different 'jobs' a councillor has to do? Write down three job titles. How well do the current job holders perform?*

▲   *3. In allocating 'jobs' to councillors, does the council make best use of their time, skills, and energies. What should be done to increase the effectiveness of councillors?*

▲   *4. How can all councillors be enabled to consider constructively the health and reputation of the council's organisation and its effectiveness as democratic local government?*

11 Making the organisation better — in practice

An organisation needs some imperative to make it change, a unifying understanding of why change is needed, a motivating vision of what its people want it to become — and strong leadership to get them there.

Demonstrated personal values, commitment and energy of the people at the top are critical, as is the need to be positive in giving confidence, support, credit, etc., in the face of the many things that go wrong.

Change must be managed — with different timescales and roles allocated to shaping the future, steering the transition and keeping necessary continuity. Major changes consume considerable time and have to be worked at on several fronts. Small changes (and the interventions to bring them about) are usually narrow and prescriptive, while major changes need a wider and more open-ended approach — and the right people in the right places to help achieve them.

Inhibitors to change

A local authority will be unlikely to change its organisation usefully unless it can tackle the purposelessness which lies at the root of some of the obstacles to good local government. We have already identified some of these obstacles:

▽ pre-occupation with point scoring not results;
▽ protection of old professional bases and career structures;
▽ line management undervalued by 'centre' elite;
▽ lack of line ownership of major management processes such as planning, resource allocation, pay and grading;
▽ general institutional inertia;
▽ crisis management.

By concentrating on the expression of the council's will, linked to its constitutional and practical responsibilities, it becomes necessary for the organisation to achieve results. The converse of these inhibitors is therefore to reorientate thinking towards the results to be achieved, towards more relevant ways of doing things, and towards different personal priorities and relationships.

Stimulants to change

Public services will always be under pressure, with finite resources and infinite demands, plus high public exposure. Since these pressures are there all the time, then they should be used to leverage change rather than allowed to induce defensiveness — the 'siege mentality' which we all know too well, together with the grim, but often perverse, holding-on to the 'known'. These are typical negative responses to the problem of tight resources and changing demands. However, the problem can be turned around if the leadership can create a different attitude of mind. Instead of being defensive externally and gloomy internally, why not promote achievement and gain public recognition which, in the doing, will generate considerable motivation within the organisation? Instead of thinking in terms of 'cuts', or reduced formal powers, why not seize the chance for shifting direction? Instead of being thwarted by the pressures, why not experiment and be extrovert in regarding this as an opportunity for changes in political dynamics? If there were such a profession as 'change agents', they would undoubtedly prefer to be plying their craft in an organisation under pressure than in one not under pressure. Organisational change is not possible without the stimulus of such things as:

▽   an external imperative, e.g. a major legislative push or resourcing challenge;
▽   new policy shifts;
▽   new and pressing communal needs;
▽   new leadership;
▽   new technology.

The paradox is that many local authorities curl up like a hedgehog against these external stimuli. Their senior employees will say 'it's taken years for us to build up this professional base, we must protect it' or 'members come and members go, so we must provide stability and continuity' — the ploy of Sir Humphrey in *Yes, Minister*.

However unhappy or uncomfortable some people may be about these stimuli, leaders ought to use and relish them as opportunities and spurs for action, not reasons for retreat. A local authority certainly does not lack for these sorts of stimuli — so how can it use them to go forward rather than backwards?

Conditions for success

The council will get nowhere by simply announcing it is going to 'reorganise'. A number of important things have to be in place first, at least so far as those who share the task of leading the council are concerned.

Especially in the value-laden public service environment, unless the leading councillors, chief executive and chief officers demonstrate their own values in their commitment to the health, purposefulness and relevance of democratic local government and to the best possible provision of services in meeting politically determined local needs, they will not establish their credentials. This is essential to do not only because it is in that way that they will eventually generate commitment externally with the public, and internally with staff, but because it is elementary tactics to ensure that one starts visibly with unimpeachable motives. Anything short of this will result in suspicions of narrow party or personal advantage and destroy widespread commitment to making the new arrangements work.

The next step for these leaders is to conceive and communicate a vision, sell it and give high profile leadership so that there can be no mistake about the vision's clarity and purposefulness, even though there may be some disagreement as to its precise content and even more as to its practical consequences. A strong message and strong leadership working from a base of integrity will be respected.

Having established that base, the next step is for the political leadership and the chief executive to create a collaborative, energetic and high-quality top team to cut through traditional territorial barriers of traditional politics and narrow professionalism which are obstructive. At this point, having done everything possible to minimise any potential vulnerability to attack from opponents, the leadership must identify and build on the strengths of other key contributors to the process of purposeful change.

If these strengths do not significantly feature people, then you will fail. You must put people first. You must select the right ones to have around you, secure their trust, motivate them, support them, keep close to them but also, over time, discriminate as to their performance; then develop and redeploy them. You must give them clear attainable objectives with freedom of action to perform. You should pick out those among them who are role models and use them as multipliers of the vision you have shared with them. You must make people feel valued; reward them and give public recognition to them for their achievements.

You must show concern for the health of the organisation and invest in it, even though it means diverting resources in order to do so. You must communicate, communicate, communicate and communicate again. Local authorities are the most people-intensive organisation bar none, and the motivation of their people has to be the single most powerful lever at your disposal. Yet how many local authorities over how many years have had agendas pre-occupied with how to achieve x% cuts in cost rather than achieving y% increase in the performance of their people?

Finally, it is vital to demonstrate practical actions and successes — which speak so much louder than words. Day by day a local authority will have enough on its plate going wrong to keep its local newspapers more than happy. So should it not plan a continuing programme of announcement of achievements, at least to its employees? Certainly if it is undergoing organisational change (which inevitably creates problems) then even more important is it to be able to signal progress achieved by employees, individually and in groups, as well as by the organisation as a whole.

If the above are some of the pre-conditions for successful organisational change, how does one manage the transition?

Accent the positive

We are often asked how to bring about organisational change 'without alienating people'. The answer is 'by motivating them'. Obviously you cannot avoid some alienation and you must seek to minimise it, but nothing will be achieved without the firm foundation of a defensible position which is focused on achieving something creditable rather than merely destroying the *status quo* and the morale of highly motivated key people who believe in what they are doing.

The positive features to communicate include:

▽   agreeing common values and objectives which bond people together;
▽   selling a vision;
▽   honouring the old ways but exchanging for the new;
▽   planning 'endings' positively — don't leave people or groups languishing;
▽   leading by example;
▽   creating local team spirit and a will to win;
▽   making successes possible and apparent;
▽   creating confidence;

▽ caring for people — including opponents;
▽ enjoying the challenge;
▽ proclaiming success;
▽ giving credit.

It will be evident that if there is not a band of people at the top of the elected and the employed parts of the organisation who embrace these attitudes, then the prospect of effective organisational change will be limited, the process dispiriting, the solutions imposed, and the prospective benefits of continuing, creative and relevant bottom-up innovation and development highly unlikely.

Making do with what you've got

All this may seem something of a utopia, but few will disagree that those are the qualities they expect in their top people. The crunch question will be, 'if you haven't got enough of these people shouldn't you bring them in?' — that is, bring in good new top people within the organisation. When approached by an authority for consultancy assistance with an 'organisation review', the first key question is whether there is a client there which potentially has the capabilities which we have been describing, or whether the call for assistance is not in fact a heavily disguised *cri de coeur* for a new chief executive or chief officer — or even (when the request comes more from officers than from members) a *cri de coeur* for an improvement in member abilities, attitudes and arrangements!

An organisational review with real ownership, commitment and a sense of adventure inside the organisation, combined with stimulating outside ideas can be tremendously powerful and rewarding — and that is the ideal we should aim for. But life isn't always like that and people have often to make do with what they have got. With skill and a fair wind it should be possible in time to get round to the key issues of quality at the top. But if it is not possible to address these issues at first, there may well be other 'ways in' — examples are given in Fig. 18. Useful individual pieces of work can be done which will also open up issues about clarity of direction, purposefulness of management and so forth. These can be built upon to expose and help to remedy the more fundamental defects of the organisation.

But if a council is genuinely concerned that it cannot answer creditably the questions set out throughout this book, then it is better by far to seek an unbiased analysis and an assessment of the reasons why their organisation is unable to formulate clear *directions*, or does not have a healthy organisation — or whatever the concern is. That analysis can be explored with the leading figures (councillors and employees) together with an assessment of the capability of the organisation to turn itself round. Clearly there will be some authorities who have a positive attitude and are willing to provide the utopian attributes explored above. In these cases the accent of an organisational review can be on the organisation itself building its *own* way forward, with such help from outside catalysts as is necessary. The consultant/client relationship in such circumstances will be a close one and the project very open ended. However, if the climate is not so helpful, e.g. because of divisions among the elected members, staff disaffection, senior incompetence etc., then the project is likely to be much more tightly prescribed both as to content, time and limitation of objective to something which is capable of a yes/no decision on implementation — which is 'voted through' and then enforced. (This tends to arise when problems are so acute and urgent that a solution has to be

'Hard'   ▽   Appoint new leader(s)
          ▽   Introduce job-related performance planning and review system
          ▽   Differentiate and align roles:
              – 'staff' support
              – 'trading' enterprises
              – 'line' management
          ▽   Conduct current job analysis:
              vs future needs to be met?
              vs job inter-relationships required?
          ▽   Review grading and pay and exit management:
              – practice
              – procedures
              – policies
          ▽   Conduct organisation resource stocktaking
              – strengths and weaknesses
              – opportunities and threats
              against assumption of where you want to be
          ▽   Conduct staff climate survey
          ▽   Conduct management effectiveness survey
          ▽   Conduct communications survey
          ▽   Management education/development programmes
'Soft'   ▽   Training needs survey

Figure 18. Organisational change: some ways in

found and hammered through quickly.) Obviously this does not feature as an ideal solution but, when needs must, there may be no alternative as a starting point for more positive developments.

Wherever a particular local authority may think it is on the spectrum of competence for handling change, it is essential that it does not just dive into an organisational review without conducting, or seeking and participating in, a survey of what the real problem is, what needs to be done about it and what the present capability is of the organisation and its people to achieve that. Careful identification of the real sources of current problems may be painful — because they usually involve some, at least, of the people responsible for providing the answers. But commissioning consultants to undertake discrete bits of technical work, unrelated to basic themes of top management, will rarely produce satisfactory results. For the outside consultant, the biggest frustration can be the client who does not know how to be a client. One only has to parody the sort of things that GPs are presented with in their consulting rooms:

> Doctor, I'm worried about this friend of mine. He seems to have these symptoms but is embarrassed to take advice . . .
> There's nothing I can do about my life-style, just give me some pills.
> It's my wife you should talk to, not me.

Figure 19 illustrates the range of different potential levels of involvement by the leaders within the organisation and any outside consultant. The key to choosing a way forward depends upon the degree of commitment and capability within the organisation to work upon and generate its own solutions.

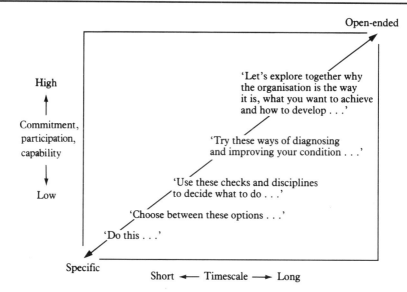

By way of illustration, this book itself operates on several levels:

▽   some peremptory assertions that something should be done with which the reader will
    not take long to (dis)agree
▽   some checklists for more studied self-diagnosis
▽   some ideas to challenge and be thought about
▽   some suggested steps which would take time and effort to work through

Care needs to be taken not to attempt long-term, fundamental change through short-term
specific interactions (unless to a wider plan) without the full commitment and skills
needed. Conversely, specific, clearly identified, short-term problems need exactly that sort
of interaction (unless planned to be remedied by a long-term change process across the
board)

Figure 19. Levels of intervention

Working back from the results you want

The usefulness of vision and clear objectives in planning a 'review' is that it
enables competing suggestions for change, and the way in which change is organised, to be evaluated in a consistent way, as well as the final results. If, for example,
a key result required of a departmental review is 'a collaborative, committed high-
quality top team providing an organisation capable of articulating and delivering
the council's priorities', then that will not only provide the criteria for judgment of
the effectiveness of the work but will necessarily inform the whole way in which
the work is designed.

Managing change

Change can only happen over time, and with different roles for different people.
Just as in the day-to-day work of an organisation there will be people who are
innovators and change agents and there are people who are good at standard operations and maintenance, so those skills can be applied in the context of organ-

isational change. Time, care and other resources have to be given to sustain the *process* of change; once initiated it must not be allowed to sink to the bottom of the agenda, suffocated by the exigencies of day-to-day pressures. The agreed vision must be important enough, and sufficiently clear and accepted, to engage these resources.

It is therefore important to have three elements of change management clearly charted, with appropriate people deployed to promote them. First, you need political leaders and a strategy to analyse and criticise the present organisation and shape the vision of what is required. Secondly, you need a steering group of top managers accountable to the leaders and strategists for the nuts and bolts of the transition process. Thirdly, you need people who can assure you that current routine operations will tick on with minimal disruption, until they are organisationally linked to the new arrangements. Thus:

▽ Positioning the organisation and shaping the change
    provide vision
    protect external boundaries   (long-term)
    appoint key people   leadership job in
    set milestones   shaping the transition
    monitor progress
▽ Managing the change elements
    new systems   (medium-term)
    new people and behaviour   'change group' of
    communications   managers
        steering the transition
▽ Keeping current operations going
    sustain former (good) values   (short-term)
    staff credibility   'continuity group'
    service delivery   assuring maximum stability

Where do you start?

One does not have to be an intellectual giant or a management guru to know whether the organisation is achieving what the council wants. Councillors are there to use intuition and common sense in judging whether the organisation's health is satisfactory. We would be surprised if councillors and senior employees reading this book have not recognised many critical themes, examples and characteristics present in their own organisation. In the Appendix which follows, we boil down everything we have said so far into a number of checklists which you can use to assess where you think your organisation is, where you would like it to get to and how you might start to change things for the better — assuming you can get enough key people to agree with you!

Questions

▲ *1. What do you think is holding your organisation back despite all the commitment, skill and energy that people put into it — inadequate people, irrelevant politics, excessive 'professionalism', or what?*
▲ *2. What changes in your council's arrangements and people would you like to see, and are they:*
very specific and quickly needed?

very profound and long term?
or where in between?

▲   *3. What should your own strategy be for getting the council and its organisation to confront and cope with the need for organisational change?*

▲   *4. Have you a potential team of colleagues:*
to give leadership for change?
to manage the transition?
to keep things going during the disruption?

▲   *5. Have you explored what outside advice and help is available, e.g. from the Local Government Training Board?*

	How well does your council . . .	Poor 1	Mar-ginal 2	Ad-equate 3	Supe-rior 4	Out-standing 5	
Conventional administration 'within the rules'	1 Assure sound administration, probity and legal process?	1	2	3	4	• 5	
	2 Resolve local problems?	1	2	3	4 •	5	
	3 Provide individual service programmes to meet statutory and local needs?	1	2	3	• 4	5	
	4 Ensure efficient management of existing means of provision and resources?	1	2	3 •	4	5	
	5 Integrate committee and departmental policies and plans internally?	1	2	• 3	4	5	
Purposeful direction and 'changing the rules'	6 Promote, coordinate and contest policies externally?	1	2 •	3	4	5	
	7 Influence locally and nationally both the public and private sectors?	1	• 2	3	4	5	
	8 Find and explore new resources?	1 •	2	3	4	5	

(Note – the dotted line is an estimate of how readers might mark this test)

Test results: Your score .... out of 40 (max.)

Your colleague's average score .... out of 40 (max.)

Comments: ....

....

Figure 20. Checklist One

Appendix — checklists

Introduction

During the whole of this book, an overriding purpose has been to engage the reader in reflection about his or her local authority and how it matches up to the various principles we have been asserting. We have provided frequent opportunities for the readers to compare and contrast their own position against basic concepts of 'organisational' arrangements for achieving results. In this Appendix we become more explicit still, providing a 'workbook' of checklists. Ideally these should not only be completed by you, but by all the key workers in the elected and the employed parts of the organisation, so that they can share together the sum of their individual responses and discuss the implications. Necessarily this will be stronger on analysis than on action, because until a clear reading is available on current organisational health and personal attitudes, and until there is the will to do something about concerns and criticism, and until there is some agreed process of reconciling and designing a way forward — then the precise objectives and means of taking action cannot begin to emerge. One of the purposes of making the book participative in this way is to enable it to be used as 'feedstock' for seminars and workshop sessions involving an individual authority's councillors and senior employees. The checklists are concerned with the following questions:

▽ Checklist One: Rating the council's performance — 'how well does your council govern?'
▽ Checklist Two: Rating the council's *directions* — 'how clear are your council's *directions* — and who sets them?'
▽ Checklist Three: Rating the council's organisational arrangements — 'how effective are your council's organisational arrangements — and how well do individuals contribute to their effectiveness?'
▽ Checklist Four: Rating the council's people — 'how good are your council's people?'

Checklist One: Rating the council's performance — how well does your council govern?

Throughout the book we have argued that local authorities in exercising their powers to provide specific services thereby have a potent means (but not the only means) of giving effect to their local priorities — their *local political agenda*. But they have no monopoly or special 'rights' to do so except on the basis of good professional performance and the bringing of demonstrable added-value because of their special local sensitivity.

	No, Never	Rarely	Occasionally	Mostly	Yes, Always
1. Does the council have a co-ordinated set of *directions* you can use? (a) with targets for priority needs? (b) with a clear financing philosophy? (c) with guidelines on generating values?					
2. Does the office's organisation provide processes and help to enable members: (a) to handle their concerns (b) to seek and evaluate information and research? (c) to resolve and articulate a majority view of their *directions*?					
3. Does the agenda management of the council and its committees focus on direction, rather than the *directions* emerging from the coincidence of several detailed decisions?					
4. Does the way in which elected members are organised or operate help the identification and agreement of the council's *directions*?					
5. Are members constructively engaged in maximising common ground and identifying crucial areas of disagreement between them?					
6. Are the *directions* of the council: (a) established 'top down' by a few members alone? (b) developed 'bottom up' by most members together?					
7. Are values (a) predominantly member driven? (b) predominantly officer driven?					
8. Are the members able to give shape priority to what they want on their agenda?					
9. Does your council in the main concern itself with macro policy rather than micro detail?					

Figure 21. Checklist Two

By implication, we were criticising the generality of councils for being hidebound within the existing system and less than fully realising their potential as genuine local governors in the widest sense of the word. Given the massive volume of local services nominally provided by local authorities, the task of their administration can take members' eyes from the wider horizon, and in the absence of clearly articulated *directions*, it becomes doubly difficult to move into a wider role concerned (as we suggest 'government' should be) with changing the rules, not just remaining bound by the *status quo* as mere administrators of 'the system'.

The detailed Checklist in Fig. 20 enables you to mark your own council's performance of its role in 'government' locally. What assessments have your colleagues made? Do ask them if your council does seem to be under-performing on any of the eight aspects of government in the Checklist, why might that be, and what should you begin to do about it?

Checklist Two: Rating the council's *directions* — how clear are your council's *directions* — and who sets them?

The council should 'own' the direction in which it is going and which it is influencing others to follow. But does it have clear, communicable *directions* which are understood by its employees, by the public, and by the councillors themselves. How much of a councillor's attention dwells on this issue as against the busy detail of 'useful daily decision-taking'? Are councillors involved in strategy-making? Are they helped by their employees to be so? Do they help themselves to be so, or do they disable each other, individually and collectively? We know the questions in Fig. 21 are not neutral; they infer some assumptions that 'local *directions*' are vital, and (in our experience) are often neglected. This can be because the urgent crowds out the important, or the traditional suffocates the novel or, worst of all, because to do so may mean actually agreeing ways forward locally across irrelevant national political divides.

Securing clear *directions* is not simple — but it is about having local integrity of view and action, about promoting collaboration as well as conflict, and about having a concern for good management. Our expectation is that, notwithstanding two decades of 'policy planning' techniques, most people will find it hard to be very positive about the way councillors establish — and are helped to establish — their council's *directions*. What do you think? Is the verdict 'must try harder'?

Checklist Three: Rating the council's organisational arrangements — how effective are your council's organisational arrangements — and how well do individuals contribute to their effectiveness?

Checklist One was about the council's fundamental role and purpose. Checklist Two was about how well the council points itself in the direction it wants to take. Let us now run a check on the capacity of the vehicle for getting there: your council's organisation and management arrangements.

Set out in Checklist Three (Fig. 22) is a distillation of the main elements of a council's organisation and management arrangements. Separate vertical columns are provided for some of the key participants, including committees and departments. You can change the names in the vertical columns, or add to them at will,

Your judgments about . . .

Local authority key tasks	Overall council effectiveness?	Individual committees' effectiveness?	Individual departments' effectiveness?
	Example: *Yours?*		
1. *Purpose* Assure integrity and purposefulness in the way the council governs and the full exercise of the authority's role and potential.	*3		
2. *Machinery* Maintain a locally appropriate means of organising and engaging members' skills and interests constructively in identifying and meeting local needs.	2		
3. *Resolution process* Ensure processes for resolving and publishing the main *directions* the council means to take, medium-term plans to achieve them and continuity of consent among members.	2		
4. *Resources* Identify, enlarge and deploy resources to provide adequate means of implementing plans.	3		
5. *Plans and programmes* Define action plans for specific results to time and budget.	4		
6. *Delegation* Give and accept accountability for results to individuals and freedom of action to achieve.	3		
7. *Operational efficiency* Secure efficient operational delivery of services whether by in-house or externally contracted resources to required results and standards.	4		

8. *Performance review* Ensure disciplined information and balanced judgment of achievement against plans, both of members and officers.	1			
9. *Corporate controls and standards* Agree (and observe) the corporate controls and standards required for self-disciplined and collaborative working, both of members and officers.	2			
10. *Effective organisation* Ensure that organisational structures, management and staffing are shaped and developed to give a cost-effective and motivated means of achieving the council's objectives.	3			
11. *External influence* Influence the government, other authorities and agencies and the community generally to gain support for the council's objectives and practical collaboration.	2			
12. *Image and reputation* Generate public understanding of the authority's purpose and performance and secure a favourable image of its integrity and efficiency, irrespective of its political postures, so that the way in which the *local political agenda* is set and met enhances rather than detracts from the role and reputation of the authority.	2			
Totals				

This is a hypothetical 'worked example' for illustrative purposes

Notes: In each column indicate level of respective contribution by marking: 5 = outstanding, 4 = superior, 3 = adequate, 2 = marginal, 1 = poor.

Figure 22. Checklist Three

in order to make individual and comparative assessments. But first take a general subjective shot at diagnosing the overall health of the authority by completing column one. What are the main strengths and weaknesses? (A hypothetical example is given for illustrative purposes.)

Plainly, some of the judgments are likely to be contentious among people in the same organisation, especially when they are made only on a basis of partial knowledge. But they provide a useful platform for starting off discussion with colleagues about the state of the machine, its capability and what may need doing to it — if it is to achieve the council's fundamental purpose, its *local political agenda*.

Checklist Four: Rating the council's people — how good are your council's people?

We have asserted in Chapter 8 the critical importance of the organisation's people — councillors as well as employees, of course. Having completed the previous three checklists and identified improvements which the council ought to be making in its performance (Checklist One), by increasing the power of its *directions* (Checklist Two) or the effectiveness of its practical arrangements (Checklist Three), we ask you to face the question 'Who will lead the council purposefully to achieve the changes needed?' This is not just about group leaders or chairmen or chief officers. It is about the contribution being made by each of the key people 'at the controls' (and who they are is for you to decide) individually and together (Fig. 23).

It is certainly not about jealousy, settling old scores or exploiting personal prejudices. It is about the jobs that need to be done well, the people most likely to do them well, and the support those people should receive. It is also about making changes at the right time and in a constructive way. These are difficult challenges which must be tackled with great care, but at least the checklist will enable you to identify the problems and begin to think of solutions as part of your own contribution to the council's leadership.

Once the most senior levels of leadership have been addressed, the demand they will make and the reliance they will place on the 'engine room' will provoke changes in the way people in the rest of the organisation are encouraged to make a useful contribution.

1. Who are the people from whom the council should expect leadership. Are they good enough for the jobs the council expects them to do?
   Put a 'YES' or 'NO' against each.

2. Where the answer is 'NO', what needs changing to put this right?
   (a) the individual job holder?
   (b) the job they have been given to do?
   (c) the organisation around them?
   (d) the (lack of) training and development they receive?
   (e) the individual's attitude, morale or motivation?
   (f) the working relationship?
   (g) what can you do to help them?

3. What should these key leaders be doing to develop 'their own' people?

4. Who is available as a replacement – and when?

5. How can a change be made in a way which best promotes the council's reputation and interests?

6. What can you do to increase your contribution, by building on your strengths and correcting your weaknesses?

7. Do you need skilled help with the 'people problems'?

8. To whom can you turn for help?

Figure 23. Checklist Four

References

1. *A Century of Municipal Progress*, 1935. Geo. Allen & Unwin, London, pp. 465–91.
2. *The Conduct of Local Authority Business*. HMSO, 1986, Cmd. 9797.
3. *The Royal Commission on Local Government in England, 1966–1969*. HMSO, Cmd. 4040.
4. At vol. 1, p. 47, para. 3.1.
5. National Conditions of Service, Section Seven, *Official Conduct*. LACSAB.
6. Committee on the Management of Local Government, HMSO, 1967.
7. Committee on the Management of Local Government. Main points of the Report, p. ix. HMSO.
8. *The New Local Authorities — management and structure*. HMSO, 1972.
9. *Getting Closer to the Public*. LGTB 1987.

Index